The Handbook of Environmental Policy Evaluation

The Handbook of Environmental Policy Evaluation

Ann Crabbé and Pieter Leroy

from Routledge

First published by Earthscan in the UK and USA in 2008

For a full list of Earthscan publications please contact:
Earthscan
2 Park Square, Milton Park, Abingdon, Oxfordshire OX14 4RN
711 Third Avenue, New York, NY, 10017, USA

First issued in paperback 2015

Earthscan is an imprint of the Taylor & Francis Group, an informa business

Copyright © Ann Crabbé and Pieter Leroy, 2008. Published by Taylor & Francis.

ISBN 13: 978-1-138-97583-5 (pbk)
ISBN 13: 978-1-84407-618-5 (hbk)

Typeset by Domex e-Data, India

Cover design by Yvonne Booth

A catalogue record for this book is available from the British Library

Library of Congress Cataloging-in-Publication Data

Crabbé, Ann.
  The handbook of environmental policy evaluation / Ann Crabbé and Pieter Leroy.
    p. cm.
  ISBN 978-1-84407-618-5 (hardback)
  1. Environmental policy–Evaluation. I. Leroy, Pieter. II. Title.
  GE170.C73 2009
  333.7–dc22
                                    2008018437

Contents

List of Figures, Tables and Boxes

FIGURES

TABLES

BOXES

About the Authors

Dr Ann Crabbé graduated in political and social sciences, specializing in public administration, from the University of Antwerp, Belgium, in 2000. She has been working as a researcher at the Faculty of Political and Social Sciences of the University of Antwerp since 2000. She obtained her PhD in 2008 with a thesis on integrated water management in Flanders, Belgium.

Dr Pieter Leroy graduated in sociology from Leuven University, Belgium, in 1976 and obtained a PhD from the University of Antwerp, Belgium, in 1983. He has been a professor of political sciences of the environment at Nijmegen University, The Netherlands, since 1994. His teaching and research activities focus primarily on the analysis and evaluation of environmental policies and politics.

Introduction

Since the 1970s, government bodies have made huge efforts to set up and implement environmental policies at levels varying from the local to the global. More recently, private businesses and non-governmental organizations (NGOs) have increasingly been engaging in environmental policies as well. Today, we witness a growing number of concerted efforts, decided upon jointly and implemented by government bodies, market agencies and representatives from civil society. Under the discursive umbrella of sustainable development, in particular, many of these efforts merge into partnerships at various scales and of various shapes. In fact, it would appear almost everybody is now engaged in environmental policy.

However, during recent years, this gradually broadening environmental field has given rise to questions concerning policies' effectiveness, as well as their efficiency, legitimacy, etc. What is more, these issues are being raised by policy-makers, but even more so by stakeholders from markets and NGOs, civil servants and academics. They may be inspired by considerations of transparency, by a concern for democracy, by the need for accountability, by the ideal of sustainability, and by other such notions. Therefore, while they all contribute to a growing interest in environmental policy evaluation, they do so for different reasons and, hence, apply different criteria.

We have witnessed this growing interest in environmental policy evaluation firsthand during our personal experiences with environmental assessment agencies, particularly in Belgium, The Netherlands and France, and also at the European level. Whether it is in the capacity of researchers, advisers or experts, we have been invited on numerous occasions to complement an environmental quality assessment with a policy assessment – that is, an evaluation of how policy contributes (or fails to contribute) to environmental quality. In other words, we have frequently been assigned to link the 'distance to targets' – whether increasing or decreasing – to policy efforts and thus to assess policy performance.

As we observed this growing demand and explored the issues at hand, we gradually became aware of two particular features of the environmental field from a policy evaluation perspective. First, while all policy areas have their own peculiarities, these are often taken into account in standard evaluation methods. Yet, although the latter have been tested and honed over many years, they might not be so readily applicable to environmental policy-making given the specific complexities of this field. Second, the expertise from the social sciences, in general, and from policy studies and policy evaluation, in particular, is still underrepresented. Most professionals in the field have not been trained in the political sciences; hence, they lack an understanding of its methodological background.

This handbook therefore aims to bridge two gaps: first and foremost, it intends to introduce the environmental policy field to a series of policy evaluation approaches. In selecting these approaches, we did not strive for academic exhaustiveness or sophistication; rather, our aim was to present them in an accessible manner, with a clear emphasis on their relevance to the environmental domain. A number of evaluative questions are formulated at the beginning of the discussion of each of the approaches in Chapters 3 and 4. These queries are real life questions encountered in the course of our research and other activities in the field. In addition, each of the approaches is illustrated with empirical cases to enhance the handbook's accessibility and relevance from an environmental policy perspective. The examples and illustrations refer to environmental policy at different levels and in various countries. While it was always our intention to gather examples from a variety of international contexts, the emphasis is, inevitably, on countries and settings with well-elaborated environmental policies and at least some experience of their evaluation.

The book's second purpose is to provide a scientifically sound, though easily accessible rather than academically sophisticated, introduction to policy studies and policy evaluation. Based on a vast academic, theoretical and methodological tradition and extensive debate, and yet avoiding academic scholasticism and excessive detail, Chapter 1 provides such an introduction. Chapter 2 addresses the environmental domain's peculiarities, with specific attention to such issues as the availability of data that are reliable and relevant to evaluation, and the long and complex cause–effect or dose–impact chains, the uncertainties that accompany these, etc. Furthermore, we pay attention to the often still sensitive issue of evaluation in the environmental field, including the role of the evaluator and possible strategies for drawing the greatest possible learning effect from an evaluation.

We trust that the present book will contribute to bridging the two aforementioned gaps. We do so, in particular, because it is based not just on our experiences as researchers; it also builds considerably on the many environmental policy evaluation meetings in which we have participated, as well as on an array of courses, workshops and other training sessions that we have organized over the years. Apart from the purely methodological issues covered in this book, there are other substantial and strategic issues to consider, including the interrelation between environmental policies and sustainability strategies; the evaluation of environmental policies in the context of their increasingly multi-actor and multi-level character; the role of evaluation within environmental assessment agencies at all levels; and the furthering of social scientific expertise within these agencies.

While we hope that this book will, in turn, provide a stimulus for new initiatives in education and training, as well as in environmental policy evaluation, we also intend it to fuel the debate on these and other important issues in the field. We would appreciate hearing about your experiences.

Ann Crabbé
Pieter Leroy
Antwerp/Nijmegen, September 2008

Acknowledgements

The authors would like to thank Michael Fell, Alison Kuznets and Hamish Ironside for their very constructive cooperation; Stephen Windross with Linguapolis for language editing; Doenja Koppejan for her assistance in updating the literature and identifying suitable empirical examples; Vanden Broele Publishers for its courtesy; and the anonymous referees for their reviews and constructive feedback to Earthscan.

List of Acronyms and Abbreviations

ADR	alternative dispute resolution
AEA	American Evaluation Association
AQS	Air Quality Strategy
BSE	bovine spongiform encephalopathy
°C	degrees Celsius
CBA	cost-benefit analysis
CEA	cost-effectiveness analysis
CIDA	Canadian International Development Agency
CIPP model	context, input, process and product evaluation model
COAG	Council of Australian Governments
CSE	case study evaluation
DDE	deliberative democratic evaluation
EA	evaluability assessment
EEA	European Environment Agency
EIA	environmental impact assessment
EIS	environmental impact statement
EMAS	Eco-Management and Audit Scheme
EPA	US Environmental Protection Agency
EU	European Union
GAM	goals achievement matrix method
GFE	goal-free evaluation
IPCC	Intergovernmental Panel on Climate Change
ISO	International Organization for Standardization
IUCN	World Conservation Union
JEP triangle	three types of evaluation criteria: juridical, economic and political criteria
LFA	logical framework approach
MCA	multi-criteria analysis
MEA	meta-evaluation/analysis
MME	mixed-method evaluation
NEPA	US National Environmental Policy Act
NGO	non-governmental organization
NORAD	Norwegian Agency for Development Cooperation
NO_x	nitrogen oxide
OECD	Organisation for Economic Co-operation and Development

PAE	popular adult education
PPBS	Programme Planning and Budgeting System
PTE	programme theory evaluation
RAPPAM	Rapid Assessment and Prioritization of Protected Area Management
RE	realistic evaluation
RIA	regulatory impact assessment
SIA	social impact assessment
SIDA	Swedish Agency for International Development Cooperation
SO_2	sulphur dioxide
UK	United Kingdom
UNEP	United Nations Environment Programme
UNESCAP	United Nations Economic and Social Commission for Asia and the Pacific
US	United States
USAID	US Agency for International Development
USDA	US Department of Agriculture
U-FE	utilization-focused evaluation

1

Policy Evaluation and Environmental Policy

The phenomenon of policy evaluation raises various questions with environmental policy-makers and with those civil servants and consultants who advise them: What is policy evaluation? How can it help (me)? How should policy evaluation be conducted? Which methods are available? The aim of this handbook is to help answer such questions in a practical way.

Anticipating the systematic presentation of a series of methods for (environmental) policy evaluation in Chapters 3 and 4, we first need to consider and to elucidate some of the basic concepts involved in policy, in policy evaluation and in the particularities of environmental policy evaluation. This chapter introduces some basic and yet fundamental concepts of policy evaluation, whereas Chapter 2 deals with the particular features of environmental policies and the specific issues that may arise from them.

The concepts and the elucidations dealt with hereafter are directly related to the actual definition of policy evaluation that is applied in this handbook: *policy evaluation is a scientific analysis of a certain policy area, the policies of which are assessed for certain criteria, and on the basis of which recommendations are formulated.*

This definition contains certain elements that are crucial to the reader's understanding of this and subsequent chapters: policy, analysis, evaluation, criteria and recommendations:

- *Policy*: while everyone has some concept of what policy is, it is worthwhile considering some frequently applied definitions, which we will do in this chapter. Depending upon how 'policy' is viewed, a different perspective emerges on the notion of policy evaluation (see Section 1.1 'What is policy?').
- *Analysis and evaluation*: in order to evaluate policy, one must first analyse it. This entails research into the what, how and why of a specific policy context. Such analytical questions always precede the actual evaluation: how effective, how fair, how enforceable and so on, is a given policy?

- *Criteria*: the essential difference between policy analysis and policy evaluation is that the latter is based explicitly on a set of specific assessment criteria. The precise nature of these criteria needs to be determined anew for each individual setting. The evolution of policy evaluation reflects a gradual change in the type of criteria applied (see Section 1.2 'Criteria for policy evaluation').
- *Recommendations*: policy evaluation is generally not an end in itself. Its purpose is, rather, to improve policy in one way or another, even when the impact of evaluation studies on actual policies is an issue in itself, which will be briefly touched upon.

Finally, we need to point out that our definition of policy evaluation implies that three types of knowledge come into play when evaluating policy: analytical knowledge, which describes and explains (what is ...?; how does ... work?; why is ...?); evaluative knowledge, which assesses (how good is ...?; how suitable is ...?); and prescriptive knowledge, which recommends alternatives (how might ... be approached differently?). This handbook focuses deliberately on methods designed to generate evaluative knowledge about policy processes, policy products and policy fields. It devotes no or very little attention to the technicalities of methods. In other words, it leaves aside questions such as how do I conduct interviews? How do I reconstruct a policy process? Nor does it touch upon methods of policy prescription, with questions such as how should I formulate recommendations? How should I test the feasibility of these recommendations? What the reader will find, though, is a broad outline of various policy evaluation methods in Chapters 3 and 4.

This chapter consists of two sections. First, light is shed on some of the key concepts: 'policy' and the different views on policy are the focus of Section 1.1; 'policy evaluation' and the various criteria involved are discussed in Section 1.2. In order to prevent the chapter from being a purely theoretical survey, we provide boxes with various well-known and less well-known definitions; give concrete examples; and point out practical problems. For the same reason, we use very few references in the chapter itself, but we provide an overview of some of the publications we have used as our main sources of inspiration at the end of the chapter. More detailed references to specific scientific literature are provided in Chapters 3 and 4.

1.1 WHAT IS POLICY?

1.1.1 The policy cycle

From the huge number of books in policy studies and policy analysis, one can draw an even greater number of definitions and concepts of policy. All of them attempt to grasp the very heart of the complexity that 'policy' represents, and to reduce its complexity by using relatively accessible and understandable models.

One of the most popular concepts in policy studies is to simplify the policy-making processes into a series of stages. This conception originates from the early days of policy analysis, and has been altered and sophisticated since, but essentially draws on a parallel with production processes. It conceives policy-making as an ongoing iteration and reiteration of a policy cycle (see Figure 1.1), in which more or less consecutive stages and the according policy processes can (analytically) be distinguished.

To further elaborate upon the policy cycle idea, we briefly discuss some of its steps:

- A number of *problems* or *societal focal points*, experienced to different degrees by people or groups, are highlighted socially and politically. In a number of cases, this may lead to the problem being placed on the *political agenda*. This is the *agenda-setting* phase. As the political agenda constantly tends to be overloaded, the existing problems are *selected* and *prioritized*. This implies that certain problems may be removed from the agenda, while others may be reformulated.

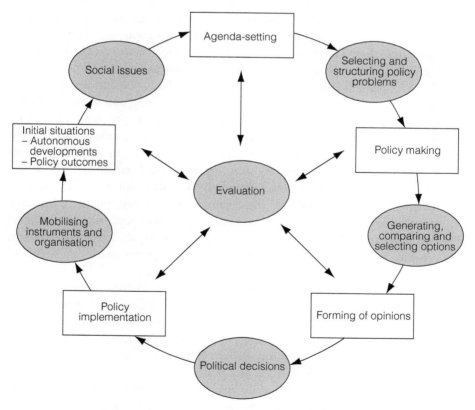

Figure 1.1 *The policy cycle*

These processes of problem definition and selection are determined by (environmental) incidents, by deliberate agenda-setting and problem definition strategies, and by the structural characteristics of the political system, which make it more sensitive to some problems than to others.

- In the *policy-making* process, solution options are developed. These solution options are presented, selected and compared in the media by interest groups, citizens and civil servants, as well as within political circles. Sometimes, scientific considerations or methods, such as cost-benefit analysis, also come into play. Opinions start to form, advocates and opponents begin to group together, and political pressure in favour of divergent solutions gradually builds up. In short, various *policy options are generated and selected*. 'Good' problem analysis and 'good' strategy formulation must, after all, promote a successful approach and its implementation. As a matter of fact, problem analysis and strategy formulation run largely parallel to one another.

- *The forming of opinions* on the remaining options takes on a more decided character. The main social and political forces adopt a position on the various solutions. This is not a 'neutral' choice, but an entirely political one: although goal-oriented, it is partly informed by political and societal viewpoints (on the role of government, the responsibilities of the business community, etc.), and, of course, by the balance of power between various social and political forces in society. This forming of opinions leads to *political decisions*, in which the basic ideas of the policy, its aims and its strategies are set out.

- The next phase is that of *policy implementation*. Basic political decisions must first be 'concretized' into specific measures: mobilizing and setting aside the required resources (manpower and budgets), specifying procedures and rules, and determining the division of tasks and the coordination between the various organizations entrusted with implementation. In sum, it involves *a mobilization of instruments and organizational planning*, the actual functioning of which is also referred to as 'policy output'. The question remains, though, whether all the resources, knowledge, power, legitimacy, etc. that are necessary for implementing the policy are, indeed, available. Furthermore, policy implementation is partly down to actors (government organizations, companies and others) who are not necessarily in favour of policy action, which entails a risk that implementation will be hindered or distorted. Policy-making is a multi-actor and a multilevel phenomenon, which partly explains the sometimes substantial differences between policy on paper and policy in practice. While the latter may be referred to as 'policy performance', the differences between ambitions and actual performance are known as the implementation deficit. This may, but need not, have a detrimental effect on the success of a policy.

- In the fifth stage, the policy *effects* manifest themselves. First and foremost, effects concern the intended changes in the behaviour of the target group (such as companies, households and motorists). This is referred to as the 'policy outcome'. Second, the term effects may refer to the intended environmental impacts (i.e. to an improvement in environmental quality). For that matter, the relationship between the two is not easy to identify. After all, a number of the outcome effects are only partly realized or not realized at all. And the end effects, the effects on the environment, are often realized only in the long run. Chapter 2 will go into these difficulties of evaluation that are partly specific to the environmental domain. In addition to these intended effects, unintended side effects may be generated that can potentially neutralize the intended effects. The controversial role of biofuels in recent debates and policies on climate change, including their unintended effects on agricultural policies, and therefore on global poverty and development, provides an example.

• In addition, while the policy process goes on, simultaneous and rather *autonomous societal developments* are occurring as well: while the environmental policy is being implemented, economic growth, individualization, globalization and other societal developments continue to unfold. Simultaneously decisions are taken in other policy fields, such as spatial planning, traffic and others, that will have an impact upon either the environmental quality or upon the target groups' behaviour. These developments, together with the outcomes of the environmental policy process itself, will lead to newly emerging social problems and therefore to renewed problem formulation and agenda-setting. In short, the policy cycle will be reiterated.

BOX 1.1 TYPES OF POLICY EFFECTS

The question of whether (environmental) policy is having an impact – many more aspects of which will be discussed below – inevitably gives rise to a counter-question: what kind of impact?

Traditionally, a distinction is made in the literature between:

• *Policy output or policy performance:* this entails the quantity and quality of the products and services delivered by policy-makers – for example, the number of permits granted, the revenue generated through environmental taxation, actual expenditures on environmental subsidies, the amount of information provided, etc.
• *Policy outcome or social change (also referred to as behavioural effect):* this comprises policy impact in terms of behavioural change among citizens, companies, farmers, consumers and other groups in society – for example, modified driving behaviour, private investment in water treatment infrastructure, increased purchases of biological products, etc.
• *Environmental impact or environmental change (also referred to as ecological impact):* examples of this include a reduction in nitrogen oxide (NO_x) or sulphur dioxide (SO_2) emissions, a decrease in water pollution or more land for organic farming.

The policy cycle is a useful concept and metaphor. After all, it reveals the different ideal-typical stages in the policy process and, in so doing, the policy-making activities that theoretically take place in each of those stages. The policy process is dissected into a kind of production process involving various sub-activities, each of which requires its own raw materials and treatment methods, as well as its own semi-finished products. This means that the activities in each of these policy stages can be methodically analysed and substantiated. What we are dealing with, then, are methods for policy development *and* for policy analysis. Many books are available in which, either for the entire policy cycle or for parts of it, various methods are described that may be used to support policy development. At the end of this chapter, a list is provided of some overview publications, while Chapters 3 and 4 refer to more specialized methodological literature.

Box 1.2 Neither *EX ANTE*, nor *EX POST*, but rather *EX NUNC*

A traditional distinction in policy evaluation is that between *ex ante* and *ex post* evaluation. The concepts are self-explanatory: *ex post* evaluation refers to the evaluation of policy after it has been developed and implemented, while *ex ante* evaluation means that policy is evaluated prior to implementation (i.e. while it is still very much on the drawing board).

Three comments are in place with regard to this distinction:

1 Methods for *ex ante* evaluation are, in fact, at once methods for policy design and policy development. Many handbooks deal with them under a single heading.
2 It is clear that *ex post* policy evaluation leads to new insights for policy development and *ex ante* policy evaluation. This learning effect, however, requires a minimum amount of *ex post* policy evaluation research that should, furthermore, provide sufficient generic (and not simply case-specific) insights. In Chapters 3 and 4 we also discuss approaches to policy evaluation in which specific attention is paid to this learning effect.
3 Most policy evaluation research is neither *ex ante*, nor *ex post*, but rather, *ex nunc* or *ex* in between, if you will: it deals with the evaluation of current policy, the interim evaluation of which may lead to modifications. Since policy is rarely completed, let alone terminated, there is very little *ex post* policy evaluation in the very strict sense of the word. Still, we will persist with the distinction between *ex post* and *ex ante*.

In the context of this book, a further aspect of the policy cycle and the position and role of evaluation is important. Many textbooks look at 'evaluation' as the penultimate stage of the policy cycle, with its final outcomes and the impact of simultaneous societal developments conceived to be the last stage. Other textbooks and our Figure 1.1, however, place 'evaluation' at the centre of the cycle, suggesting that each phase of the policy cycle may be evaluated. The methods we list in Chapters 3 and 4 differ in many respects, including that some of them are appropriate to one or, in particular, several of the policy cycles' evaluation. It might be clear, indeed, that policy evaluation questions may relate to each or to several of these phases. By way of illustration, we consider some environmental policy problems with examples of evaluative questions about successive stages of the policy cycle:

- *Problem formulation: livestock manure.* From the late 1970s until today, different European countries have faced environmental problems related to intensive livestock farming (i.e. problems of increasing volumes of manure). From international comparative research on this period, it is clear that these problems have been defined successively as a non-issue, a regional surplus, a processing problem and a matter of volume control. For domestic reasons, varying from a country's physical geography to the power relations between its main stakeholders, the problem has further been defined in terms of water pollution, acidification, an odour problem, a technical problem within the agricultural sector, etc.

    From a policy evaluation point of view, this raises interesting questions as to how the prevailing problem formulation has affected the subsequent phases of the policy development process and, ultimately, the effectiveness of this policy. In other words, a legitimate evaluative question could be: to what extent was the prevailing formulation of the livestock manure problem adequate (appropriate, consistent, complete, etc.) in order to pursue an effective policy?

- *Problem formulation/selection: the role of public perception.* Under normal conditions, environmental policies and their risk assessment are assumed to be formulated by experts. They tend to present risks in terms of probabilities and impacts. Under situations of environmental crisis, though, public perception, echoed by the media and parts of the political system, tend to have a huge societal and political impact. Risks related to the environment, food safety and public health, although assessed to be small by experts, may then be magnified as examples from the BSE crisis ('mad cow' disease), foot-and-mouth disease and others illustrate.

    From an evaluative point of view, this raises questions on the respective roles of social perception and scientific information in assessing an environmental problem, its formulation, its priority on the agenda, and its impact on the actual policy measures taken.

- *Instrumentation: wastewater policies.* Almost all countries on the globe face more or less huge wastewater problems. The way in which they deal with it is quite different, of course, in terms of their geographical, environmental, economic and political situation, as well as their capacities. However, these political responses will also differ with regard to their basic strategies: do these responses predominantly rely on regulatory strategies, economic instruments, or public or private investments and efforts, etc.? The strategies adopted are partly inspired by considerations of effectiveness and efficiency; but no doubt these have also been determined by domestic institutional conditions, such as the role and position of the state and its different administrative levels, as well as the role of water companies, private investors, etc.

In terms of policy evaluation, an intriguing series of possible questions rises: to what extent has the choice of instrumentation strategies been inspired by institutional needs and by the pre-existing organization of the policy domain, rather than by considerations related to effectiveness? In other words, is the instrumentation of the policy that was opted for the most appropriate (effective, suitable, legitimate, accepted, etc.)?

These (real life) examples highlight just a few of the policy evaluation questions that may be formulated in each stage of environmental policy-making processes. Chapters 3 and 4 contain a variety of methods, some of which specifically focus on a particular stage of the policy cycle, in some cases also with specific methods. As might be clear from these examples, however, many of the evaluative questions can only be answered adequately if one analyses and assesses a much larger part of the policy cycle.

While this demonstrates that, as a concept, the policy cycle definitely has its merits, its simplicity can also be misleading. More specifically, it may create the impression of not being an ideal-typical representation, but rather an accurate reflection, or even a normative standard, of reality. As far as we are concerned (and in the context of this book), the policy cycle is no more than a heuristic or analytical tool. In no way do we wish to imply that processes of policy-making actually unfold according to these (chrono)logical steps, nor, indeed, that they ought to. There is sufficient empirical evidence from policy studies to falsify any of these suggestions. Furthermore, the notion of the policy cycle, like any schematic representation, tends to accentuate some, and to ignore other, parts and characteristics of policy reality. The following section considers varying answers as to what policy is, or at least how it could be conceived; from there, it relates divergent views to (environmental) policy evaluation.

1.1.2 Policy: Three different views, three types of evaluation

The questions of what policy is and how it can be approached have given rise to much debate in policy studies. Consequently, many scientific publications on the subject carry titles such as 'Views on policy' or 'Public policies: Competing paradigms'. Even in everyday language, various definitions of policy are used, which again are based on different perceptions and views. We do not intend to provide an extensive overview of these discussions in policy theory and practice, but merely to discuss three clearly distinguishable views on policy, each of which implies a different perspective on policy evaluation and its functionality. The views that we discuss are 'policy as a control loop', 'policy as political interaction' and 'policy as an institutional phenomenon'. We provide a brief outline of each perspective and its implications in terms of policy evaluation.

Policy as a goal-oriented rational-synoptic process

In the first conception, policy is seen as a process of conscious and rational problem-solving. In policy cycle terms: a social problem has become a policy problem as a result of a process of agenda-setting, with a clear problem definition and consequent goal-setting, on the basis of which different policy options are developed. These options are compared and weighed against each other in some sort of multi-criteria evaluation, after which one or a combination of them is selected and implemented. At the end of the process, a policy evaluation can assess whether, or to what extent, the initial problem has been resolved, and whether or not the policy cycle must be reiterated.

In this view, policy is like a control loop. It is a concept borrowed from the simple principles of process technology and engineering sciences, the household thermostat being a well-known example. When set at 20°C, the thermostat will detect 'a problem' at 19°C (i.e. a difference between the actual and desired situation). This elicits a signal: 'heat on'. Consequently, heat is produced and transported through the system, heat exchange ensues and the room temperature rises. Once the desired room temperature has been reached, 'heat off' is signalled and the problem has been solved. Should the problem reappear, the process will be repeated. In short, the control loop resembles a fully automatic operational process, with feedback of information resulting in task modification.

No policy scientist takes the control loop metaphor too literally. There are, however, many policy scientists – and even more policy practitioners – who tend to regard policy-making as a process that is driven mainly by a problem-solving rationale. In this view, policy is approached as a means of rationally tackling social problems. The word 'rational' refers, first and foremost, to the method: effective and efficient strategies are sought on the basis of scientific methods. Multi-criteria analysis and other approaches of *ex ante* policy evaluation are ascribed a major, if not decisive, role in these processes. 'Rational', secondly, refers to the motives and the nature of the parties involved: these parties are rational beings, who – like *Homo economicus* – calculatingly look for the best possible solutions. In short, this concept of policy is strongly influenced by engineering and by economic thought, and elaborated upon in rational choice theories in different social science disciplines.

Seen from this perspective, the purpose of policy evaluation is quite clear: policy must essentially be assessed and optimized using the criteria of goal attainment and suitability, often played out in a series of clear-cut indicators. Conversely, a great many practical evaluation questions that policy-makers put forward are, often rather implicitly, aligned with this engineering-inspired view of policy-making, restricting any assessment and evaluation of their work to the monitoring of a set of indicators. They are, after all, concerned with identifying the best (i.e. most rational) way of analysing, tackling and solving the policy problem. In other words, policy evaluation is intended to contribute to the further rationalization of policy.

Policy science has a large number of methods at its disposal to help answer the kind of policy evaluation questions originating from this perspective. Let us consider some examples, relating to three different policy phases:

1 *Reconstruction of policy theory.* Policy is invariably based on certain assumptions regarding the causes of the problem to be addressed, the solution strategies to be pursued and the underlying ethics and moral principles. These assumptions are largely implicit: if they are made somewhat more explicit in policy documents, then this is usually not equivocal. The European Water Framework Directive gives a recent example of a policy document that explicitly lists a series of principles – although very differently elaborated upon and 'operationalized', and without addressing the possible and actual contradictions between them. As a consequence of the often implicit character of these policy principles, the evaluator needs to reconstruct them. Such reconstruction of underlying assumptions generally reveals inconsistencies ('irrationalities') in analysing the problem, the solution strategies and the premises, and identifies ways of rectifying these shortcomings. Drawing up so-called target trees or goal mean trees are commonly applied tools to check policy assumptions for their validity and reliability. The aim of this type of policy evaluation is to upgrade the quality of policy assumptions to a scientific (i.e. to a more rational) level.

2 *Predicting effect and effectiveness.* A rational approach to a policy process implies a prior (*ex ante*) estimation of the likelihood that the intended effects will actually be attained. Using a wide range of methods of forecasting, impact assessment and the like, an attempt is made to predict the effects and, consequently, the effectiveness of a policy. Crucial in this respect is the assessment of the likelihood that the target group (e.g. individual motorists, a group of local communities or companies) will change its behaviour, and an appraisal of the degree of regulation, financial stimulation or public information required in order for such a change to take place. Depending upon the field of study (economics, public administration, psychology, etc.), the approaches differ; but their common aim is to establish which type of tool should preferably be deployed and which 'dose' should be administered to achieve the desired

'effect'. This approach, too, is based on a rational view of policy-making as one assumes people and organizations to be sensitive to a change in the balance of wins and losses, and to adapt their behaviour accordingly.

3   *Gauging effectiveness.* In this perspective on policy-making, problem-solving is the driving mechanism and the ultimate, sometimes exclusive, criterion for assessment. Thus, *ex post* effectiveness evaluations are clearly the polar opposite of *ex ante* evaluations. A whole repertory of methods is available for answering the effectiveness question, especially from a cost-benefit and, even more so, a cost-effectiveness point of view.

From a rational perspective on policy, two issues are extremely important here: the problem of the causal connection between policy efforts (the 'dose') and their (different types of) effects, on the one hand (see Box 1.1 on the different types of policy effects; see also Box 1.3 on causality), and the problem of side effects, on the other. Here too, various methods are available, both quantitative and qualitative in nature. However, given its premise of rationality, this approach will usually show a preference for quantitative methods.

The perspective whereby policy is seen as a control loop is tempting, particularly its simple basic assumptions and transparency: people observe a problem and decide to tackle it by means of a well-considered policy intervention. Consequently, it should be easy to determine whether that intervention has been successful or needs to be repeated or modified.

At this point, however, it might be clear that this rational view of policy and the metaphor of the control loop entail certain limitations, resulting from their specific conception and reduction of reality. First and foremost, the premises of the 'rational actor theory' are only tenable to a limited degree. The actions of human beings and organizations may be (and actually are) guided by considerations other than those that are rational and goal-oriented. Second, the notion that policy is driven mainly by the desire to solve problems is an idealistic distortion: a whole array of driving forces may come into play in problem formulation, agenda-setting and prioritization, as well as in the implementation of decisions. These range from moral indignation to emotions, from power imbalances to monopoly situations, from private interest to prestige, from policy tradition to disputes over competencies. All of these considerations, motives and contextual factors, regarded as 'irrational' from a strictly rational point of view, do play their role in policy-making, in general, and in environmental policies. This, in part, explains why official policy goals almost never coincide with real, but often difficult to detect, ambitions. Third, by approaching policy-making as a control loop, one effectively ignores part of the reality in the analysis. The one-sided emphasis on the solution-focused nature of policy-making overlooks other aspects, one of which is the fact that policy is not a fully automatic process or control loop, but is, rather, created in an environment of continuous social and political interaction. This brings us to the second perspective on policy-making.

BOX 1.3 THE QUESTION OF CAUSALITY

A political and methodological focal point in policy evaluation, where the evaluator tries to gain insight into the degree of effectiveness, is the main focus of causality. By this we mean that one strives to (positively) answer the question of whether the intended policy effects (the goals) have actually been achieved thanks to the policy.

This sounds much easier than it is. After all, a policy may attain its goals due to favourable external circumstances, or due to the impact of another policy, or because of a foreign influence. A reduction in polluting emissions may be the result of a flagging economy rather than an effect of environmental policy. Policy-makers, in general, tend to attribute policy failure to situations abroad or to 'external circumstances', while they tend to claim responsibility for policy successes themselves.

The difference between goal attainment and effectiveness lies precisely in the causal role of policy. Thus, it is imperative that an evaluation of policy effectiveness is conducted with care and accuracy. However, this is complicated in various ways:

- Policy aims are often unclear, sometimes deliberately vague and difficult to measure so that it is impossible to ascertain unequivocally that the goals have been attained.
- Policy rarely consists of one measure – a so-called single shot – but usually encompasses a whole series of measures, making it difficult to assess the effect and effectiveness of the policy.
- The policy path, from policy formulation to policy outcome, passes along many links and through numerous actors. Chapter 2 discusses the multi-actor and multilevel features of contemporary policy-making. Moreover, especially in the case of environmental policy, there can be a substantial time lag, another specific feature that Chapter 2 addresses. Groundwater quality and halting biodiversity loss are self-evident domains that illustrate the huge time delay between policy efforts and their eventual effects. Consequently, causal chains are long so that it becomes tricky to identify crucial factors.

For all of these reasons, 'pure' examples of effectiveness evaluation are scarce. This explains why one particular example always stands out, including at the European level (EEA, 2001): the effectiveness of initially phasing out and subsequently banning leaded petrol is entirely quantifiable, down to the end effect of 'amount of lead in verges'. It is an exceptional example because it concerns a single substance, a single sector of industry, a limited number of measures taken over a limited period of time, and a fairly simple, natural pattern of diffusion. The effectiveness in terms of public health impact, however, is much trickier to calculate because it involves a much more complex set of influences and outcomes.

Policy-makers find it hard to accept that the question of causality can only be answered in exceptional cases. Consequently, research into policy evaluation is constantly searching for methods to describe the effects and the effectiveness of policy, despite all of the pitfalls such an undertaking inevitably involves. Chapters 3 and 4 illustrate the divergent responses that literature has given to this challenge. In fact, one invariably tries to make plausible what the effects and the effectiveness of policy are (or have been) through indirect reasoning and argument. The latter comes close to what is called 'circumstantial evidence' before a court of law.

Another aspect of policy-making that is neglected is the fact that policy-making unfolds in a pre-set institutional context. This latter point brings us to the third perspective on policy making.

Policy as political interaction

Whereas the previously discussed view on policy is strongly inspired by engineering and economic thought, and by a rational actor model, the 'policy as interaction' perspective we discuss here is more inspired by paradigms from political sciences, in which policy is mainly the product of power relations between various social and political actors, groups, convictions and interests. In other words, whereas in the first view, policy is regarded as a matter of rationally designing and implementing a problem-solving strategy, in the second, it is seen mainly as an unfolding struggle between conflicting interests and power bases.

This view on policy, too, can be elucidated by passing through the successive links in the policy cycle. In doing so, the differences will become clear, not only in relation to the policy view, but also in terms of questions about, and expectations of, policy evaluation:

• *Agenda-setting*: if policy is seen as political interaction, the questions of whether and how social problems can be placed on the agenda depend mainly upon the capability of the various social and political actors to push through 'their' issues and problem definitions. This capability, in turn, depends partly upon the actors' own resources in terms of expertise, personnel, financial and other means, and partly upon the political context in which the policy unfolds. Thus, the previously mentioned successive shifts in the formulation of the livestock manure problems in different countries may reflect the changing balance of power between the actors involved in a context in which, in many countries, there used to be a privileged relationship between the ministry and the farming industry. While in some countries the manure issue has led to the breakthrough of this neo-corporatist policy-making style and practice, other countries witnessed the successful survival of a rather closed agricultural–environmental policy domain. Empirical research in different countries illustrates the relation between the balance of power and the interactions between the stakeholders involved, on the one hand, and the way in which the problem is formulated and handled in the consecutive stages of the policy cycle, on the other.

In order to analyse and evaluate policies from this perspective, one could rely on different models of agenda-setting and issue-handling – for instance, the barrier model – suggesting that successful agenda-setting implies conquering a number of barriers which selectively block access to the political agenda, or the policy streams approach, suggesting that agenda-setting depends upon bringing together problem definitions and solution options, and upon seizing windows of opportunity. These and other approaches emphasize the capacities of political agencies to mobilize resources and to seize opportunities for the sake of agenda-setting, or they point to the institutional context that offers such opportunities or, rather, blocks these. Any of these approaches can provide insight into who has succeeded in imposing a problem definition and, as the case may be, into associated solution strategies, which power tools have been decisive in this regard, etc. This perspective also provides insight into why, in certain cases, issues are denied or removed from the political agenda, and why no policy response takes shape even if some recognize there to be a clear social issue. The latter might be related, for instance, to the respective impact of experts' assessments versus lay people's evaluations, particularly in some crisis circumstances, which we referred to earlier. In brief, it is not its problem-solving orientation or its 'rationality', but, rather, the way in which the problem formulation reflects political and societal interaction that is at stake in policy evaluation.

• *Policy formation*: if one regards policy as a process of political interaction, the crucial question in this phase is not whether and how the selection of policy options and, ultimately, of a policy strategy, can be reasoned and optimized on the basis of the problem solution. The question is, rather, how this selection process should involve negotiations between the various actors concerned and, conversely, how the approach chosen should reflect the problem perception and solution paths of these actors, as well as the relationships between them. From this perspective, again, the policy goal is not so much the result of an ambition to resolve a problem, but rather a reflection of the power balance between the actors involved. These actors may be political, economic and social interest groups, as well as government agencies, which must themselves promote their viewpoints and fight for authority, resources and influence. If policy comes about in such a multi-actor setting, where different perspectives and interests must vie for influence and power, the question arises how such a tangle of interaction and intrigue may be woven into a compromise.

As far as policy analysis and policy evaluation are concerned, approaches such as network analysis, power relations and power-balance analysis, stakeholder mapping, and the like offer useful frameworks for explaining and assessing policy choices, including understanding the success or failure of these choices. According to this view, policy evaluation is no longer limited to comparing goals with achieved effects. It is, in other words, no longer seen merely as an assessment of policy products (output). This doesn't mean, however, that policy evaluation from this perspective need not be restricted to an evaluation of the policy process, particularly the interactions between those involved. Instead, policy evaluation from this perspective should be able to scrutinize the connection between the policy process and the policy organization, on the one hand, and its very outcome – the substantial policy product – on the other. Much attention is devoted to the manner in which the actors, either under the guidance of government or through other facilitators, mediators or policy brokers, organize the policy process, and whether the chosen approach is suitable for connecting contradictory interests. In other words, one explores which policy organization and processes are suitable or not for the so-called interweaving of goals. In addition, the evaluation may focus on the acceptance and workability of the results achieved. After all, there are examples of unworkable as well as extremely successful compromises. From a policy development point of view, it can be interesting to investigate *ex post* which circumstances of policy process organization and implementation play a role in this respect.

- *Policy implementation*: according to the rational view on policy-making, the implementation of policy is conceived as a politically neutral process. This results in policy evaluations that investigate where, how and why implementation stalls, and why this was not anticipated more effectively.

  If one regards policy as a form of political interaction, however, policy implementation is 'the continuation of decision-making by other means'. Seen from this perspective, policy implementation is a process in which a variety of decisions need to be constantly made, and throughout which power, acceptance, information, capacity and other elements play a decisive role. The policy implementers, who from a rational point of view are seen too readily as fully automated signal relayers, are now viewed as actors with their own goals and ambitions, who are able to carry out or oppose policy decisions from elsewhere, who may or may not possess the resources to do so, etc. Thus, policy can be evaluated in terms of the degree to which it possesses the means of facilitating or obstructing implementation (or, as the case may be, having it obstructed).

  In this respect, policy studies and policy evaluation literature recently paid a lot of attention to implementation processes that ask for the interplay between government bodies at different administrative levels: the formal and material implementation of international agreements (e.g. on climate change and biodiversity) is one example; the interaction between national and local authorities reveals similar mechanisms of implementation as a multilevel game. This conception of policies as a multilevel game implies that, again, interaction between a multitude of actors is seen as the key factor in explaining successes and failures of policy processes.

It should be clear from the above that while the perception of policy as a form of political interaction is certainly a more realistic representation of policy-making, it does not make policy evaluation any easier. The increased realism lies in the following aspects:

- There is now room in the policy evaluation for dealing with other, entirely different, motives than those focused on in the rational model. This results in a less one-sided and more complete picture of reality.

Box 1.4 Policy: Goal-oriented or goal-seeking? Some consequences for evaluation

From a rational perspective, one would assume that policy is goal-oriented. This implies that there is a clear and unambiguous problem definition and solution strategy – which, in reality, is seldom the case – on the basis of which the policy effects can be gauged. In other words, according to this viewpoint, the policy itself provides the criteria against which it is to be assessed.

The fact that policy is regarded as the result of interaction not only means that more attention is paid to the process, but also that policy is seen to be goal-seeking rather than goal-oriented. The latter is especially the case in those policy processes that use interaction as an essential means of getting policy processes moving. This is the case in many, often regional, processes under mobilizing but rather vague umbrellas, such as 'sustainability', in which government bodies, market players and all kinds of societal organizations interactively aim at designing and implementing an appropriate policy for a specific region or for resolving a series of interrelated issues.

When evaluating this type of policy, process evaluation must, of course, play an important role. Traditional methods of gauging effectiveness are largely useless in this respect since there is no clear-cut goal definition – or, when there is one, it may shift over time as interactions go on. A policy evaluation of these processes is likely to be more successful when it is designed interactively and is participatory. Such an evaluation can also involve feedback, not only with regard to the actors' satisfaction with the process, but also whether the actors feel their ambitions and goals are reflected in the end result.

Chapters 3 and 4 discuss forms of participatory evaluation. As we will see, newer variants of environmental policy-making (interactive, participatory, deliberative, etc.) have greatly contributed to the development of this approach to policy evaluation. In turn, participatory designs for policy evaluation might help, in these circumstances, to overcome the limitations of 'rational' designs.

- There is also room for evaluating the policy process, particularly the way in which it enables and structures interactions between those involved, as an important explanatory variable for goal attainment and the suitability of policy.

As a consequence, however, policy evaluation seems more complex:

- From this perspective, policy evaluation in terms of goal attainment and effectiveness is no longer sufficient. In addition to these criteria, we must now also deal with conditions such as acceptability, legitimacy and participation, which are primarily intended to help assess the process. This implies a complication: policy may be rational; but it is so rarely accepted that it is not implemented and, consequently, remains ineffective. Conversely, weak policy processes may result in effective policy. In other words, criteria for policy evaluation may yield contrary results. Section '1.2 Criteria for policy evaluation' deals in more detail with the issue of criteria and the contradictions between them.

- In many cases, particularly if there is lengthy interaction and cumbersome political decision-making, policy evaluation in terms of goal attainment or efficiency is virtually out of the question. Such a situation tends to arise when policy goals are vague, ill formulated or frequently reformulated. Lasting interactive processes at regional level, dealing with complex and interwoven issues such as agricultural developments, nature conservation, water management, spatial planning, housing and tourism, clearly illustrate the case. Policy evaluation from the perspective of policy as a control loop occasionally tends to ignore such complications.

In Chapters 3 and 4 it will gradually become clear that almost all methods of policy evaluation, and especially the most classical and robust ones, are in keeping with the first perspective: policy as a 'simple' control loop. Policy evaluation based on the perception of policy as political interaction is more complex; consequently, fewer methods, particularly standardized ones, are available.

Policy as an institutional phenomenon

The third perspective on policy further inspires the policy evaluation process, but also makes it more complex. The perceptions of policy as a control loop and as a form of political interaction primarily explore specific, often more or less separate, policy processes in the here and now. Such evaluations generally relate to the contents, the organization and implementation of a single policy intervention. There are two reasons for the emphasis in policy evaluation on the here and now, as well as the focus on processes that are regarded more or less irrespective of their context: one is political and the other is scientific in nature. First, policy evaluation research is often commissioned research and clients are mainly interested in short-term assignments dealing with specific policy efforts. Second, from a methodological point of view, it seems only natural that scientists should have a preference for policy processes that can be evaluated more or less separately since such processes are often the easiest to assess.

This approach, however, also has its limitations: real life day-to-day policy processes do not unfold in isolation, but rather as a part of a broader, relatively stable framework of policy-making, often referred to in literature as policy subsystems, policy regime, etc. – concepts that, quite rightly, express the stability or continuity of the patterns of behaviour, the styles and practices in a specific policy domain. Indeed, policy fields and domains over the years have established ways and styles of policy-making that may have become rigidly institutionalized. This is what has earlier been referred to as the pre-existing institutional context in which a specific policy process unfolds, and by which that process, to a lesser or greater extent, is pre-structured and characterized.

Be that as it may, the institutionalized manner of policy-making is certainly related to the dominant view of one's own policy field and the central tasks

Box 1.5 Institutionalization and Policy

The notion of institutionalization is a basic concept in social sciences that essentially refers to the phenomenon that human behaviour gradually becomes fixed in its responses and actions. Ideals, norms and opinions, on the one hand, and practices and ways of going about things, on the other, slowly converge in broadly shared views that need no further explanation; in fixed operational methods that are accepted and adopted by all; and in rules and structures that would appear to be undisputed. Much of so-called individual behaviour is thus entrenched in 'institutional behaviour': at school, at work and at home, we display and expect others to display certain types of behavioural patterns. Although we seldom discuss them explicitly, we are well aware of the norms and rules that come with these patterns, and this gives us confidence and a sense of security. Institutions thus legitimize and stabilize social interaction.

All of the above applies equally well to policy-making. The contents and organization of policy, too, are gradually fixed in specific patterns; in common perceptions of the policy problem at hand; in conceptions of the main mission and characteristics of the policy field involved, as well as its boundaries with adjacent fields; and in accepted views of who the principal players are, what the balance of power between these players is, and how they interact. Thus, many policy fields are characterized by more or less fixed definitions of problems, by more or less fixed relationships between the actors involved, and by more or less fixed ways of policy-making and policy implementation.

Policy scientists differ in the degree to which they focus on the institutionalization of policy, how significant they find it and how they interpret both the construction and the impact of these institutional features. As a result, they refer to them in different terms. Some policy scientists emphasize the lasting predominance of historically established institutions, and focus on path dependency and other phenomena of historical institutionalism. Others emphasize the fact that institutions constantly need to be renewed as their legitimacy is challenged by new ideas and new developments. The position of national environmental policies in a gradually globalized context is such a challenging issue. Furthermore, some scholars emphasize the existence of 'discursive coalitions' to indicate the far-reaching and often lasting discursive unanimity within a policy domain field; others talk about 'regimes' to highlight regulatory aspects. It is worthwhile, for instance, evaluating to what extent the European Habitats Directive would have changed discourses and coalitions at national level in different member states. Other scholars prefer to use the concept of 'networks' to emphasize the strong connections between the actors involved; while yet others use the concept of 'institutional arrangements' to point out the close ties between policy contents and policy organization. Finally, some refer to the concept of 'policy style' to characterize the more or less fixed way of policy conduct in a specific field.

involved; of the relationships between the principal actors; of the distribution of funds, knowledge and power; of the style in which people or groups of people deal with one another; of the manner in which policy is implemented; of the relationships with local authorities or quasi-autonomous administrative bodies; etc. When a civil servant who has been transferred to a different policy field says something like: 'Water policy is, of course, completely different from waste policy', it is often these kinds of features that he or she is referring to. Also relevant in this context is the manner in which a policy field reacts to new events; to the way in which scientific input is ensured; to the way in which the interaction with the market and civil society is organized; and so on. The latter characteristics, in fact, refer to what can be labelled as organizational flexibility, which, in turn, largely explains the learning capacities of institutions and organizations. And 'learning', as we will see, could or should be a major outcome of policy evaluation.

It is hard to identify the institutional features of a policy field or subfield (e.g. the institutional characteristics of waste management, water policies or nature conservation and biodiversity) without a clear point of reference. More or less theoretically constructed typologies are helpful; but quite often scholars do carry out empirical comparisons. In general, there are essentially three ways of comparatively describing the characteristic institutionalization of a policy field: an international comparison between two similar policy fields, thus taking an international comparative perspective; a national comparison between two policy fields, often called a cross-sector approach; and a comparison between a specific policy field 20 years ago and today: a longitudinal comparison. Each of these methods is labour intensive and time consuming.

Two real life examples might clarify the case policy evaluation from an institutional perspective. The first relates to the policy evaluation question as to why organic farming, in some countries at least, has thus far achieved only a very modest market share, well below the stated policy goals. Such an evaluative question cannot be answered adequately if, from a rational actor point of view or from a policy as interaction perspective, one considers just a single or a few policy interventions: some regulatory measures, some economic incentives and a series of communicative efforts to endorse organic farming and the distribution and consumption of its products. From an institutional perspective, one requires, instead, an evaluation of the:

- institutional features of organic and traditional farming;
- institutionalized practices within the production, distribution and consumption chains;
- logistical, financial, scientific and technological support offered to the respective sectors.

In other words, such an evaluation requires an analysis of the institutional context, rather than an analysis of the impact of this or the other policy measure.

The second real life example concerns an evaluation as to why scientific research, including deliberately policy-oriented research, in the environmental field – or an associated subfield – has had such a limited impact upon environmental policy-making. This question again cannot be adequately answered on the basis of an evaluation of individual research projects and their valorization (or lack thereof). What is required is an analysis of the institutional organization of knowledge production, and how it is stimulated and applied, including the operational approaches and styles in the field, etc. What can be explored is whether traditional ways of knowledge production and use, or old 'knowledge arrangements', obstruct more contemporary approaches. Only this type of evaluation can yield recommendations for a reorganization of the entire policy field of environmental knowledge. And only this kind of reorganization of the context can lead to a policy conduct that brings the attainment goals closer.

Based on this kind of research, policy scientists have discovered just how stable and lasting some of these institutional patterns are, how they are continually being reproduced and consolidated, and how resistant they are to change. In certain cases, stability can turn into inertia or rigidity, and this, in turn, may leave a policy field ill equipped for tackling a new policy problem. After all, the latter is likely to necessitate an approach that does not fit in (well) with existing policy tradition or policy context. In terms of policy evaluation, if policy processes are not attuned to the context or vice versa, then the chances of achieving effective policy are greatly compromised. On the other hand, though, the environmental policy field (since it is still young compared to others, and quite constantly challenged with new issues and developments) displays rather high institutional dynamics. Air pollution during the 1970s turned into acidification in the 1980s, and into climate change and concern over particulates over the last decades. Not only do we witness major shifts in the problem formulation, these are paralleled with new policy strategies and new organizational forms, underpinned with scientific expertise from other disciplines, etc. Similar challenges are to be witnessed in fields such as nature conservation, with conservation work evolving into biodiversity policies, water policies evolving into integrated water management, corporate environmental management broadening into corporate social responsibility, etc. In all of these cases, new problem formulations create new goals, strategies and organizations, while the increasing globalization and Europeanization of these environmental domains simultaneously encourage reorganization – in other words, we witness institutional challenges here that ask for institutional responses.

It is clear to see that at the heart of this institutional perspective lies the question of what the typical features of a certain institutional context are and how they affect specific policy processes and policy products. The quintessence of an institutional evaluation is to know whether that institutional context is suitable and adequately equipped for the type of policy one intends to pursue. And the ensuing recommendations will relate to the type of institutional context that is best or better suited for that type of policy. In other words, recommendations assume the form of an institutional design.

These questions are not easy to answer and the type of recommendations referred to are challenging to formulate. As a matter of fact, policy evaluations at an institutional level are forced to build on an array of evaluations at lower, more concrete, levels. At the same time, it is clear that they reveal structural causes of policy success or policy failure and seek out practical reasons for improving policy. But, again, the methods of institutional policy evaluation are less robust and have not been as extensively tested, so they will not be studied in great detail in the subsequent chapters.

1.2 CRITERIA FOR POLICY EVALUATION

At the beginning of this chapter, we defined policy evaluation as *a scientific analysis of a certain policy area, the policies of which are assessed for specific criteria and on the basis of which recommendations are formulated.*

In order to demonstrate that policy evaluation can be approached from several angles, the first section dealt with the question: what is policy? The answer to this question was that, starting from three different perspectives on policy and policy-making, policy evaluation may be evaluated from three different perspectives as well: as a control loop, as a form of political interaction and as an institutional phenomenon. We can easily imagine these perspectives as three levels of analysis. Which level of analysis is used obviously depends upon the policy evaluation question that is being addressed. In turn, and less obvious, is the conclusion that any policy evaluation question thus (even unintended) fits into a certain perspective – and therefore has to be assessed according to its suitability. In addition, we noted that as we move from the first perspective to the third, increasingly fewer tested methods of research are available. This is why, in Chapters 3 and 4, we focus on policy evaluation methods that approach policy as a rational goal-oriented process and as a form of political interaction. However, with regard to certain issues, perspectives for institutional evaluation will be outlined.

In this section we deal with the question: what are the criteria against which policy is to be evaluated?' A short historical outline leads us to three main sets of criteria, which we subsequently relate to the internationally formulated criteria of 'good governance'.

1.2.1. A brief history of policy evaluation and criteria

Policy evaluation, only recently gaining popularity in the environmental field, is much older than many people think. As the governance of national states grew increasingly complex during the course of the 19th century, national parliaments found themselves barely able to carry out their task of checking the executive branch of government. They lacked the expertise to comprehend the intricate mix of government budgets, income and expenditure, and annual accounts, let alone to evaluate them. Against this backdrop, audit offices or comparable bodies were established in almost all parliamentary democracies in order to provide support to national parliaments. In some cases, they were re-established because audit offices had, in fact, been around in some European early-modern cities and kingdoms in various forms. The successive competencies and responsibilities that these audit offices held offer some excellent general insights into the development of national states, and their views on, and practices of, governance, democracy and control, leading to the development of policy evaluation.

Likewise, the successive criteria that were emphasized within the monitoring (i.e. the evaluative role of these audit offices) are extremely instructive. Traditionally, audit offices, in their capacity of special advisers to the legislative branch of government, were (and still are) responsible for monitoring whether government policy is lawful, whether the budgets are being used for the purposes they were intended for, etc. These criteria bear witness to the traditional, mainly statutory, debate on the role of the state, the state's right to levy taxes and draw up public budget, and citizens' right to protection against the arbitrariness of that same state. In this context, it is understandable that this form of 'policy evaluation' focuses strongly on mainly legally inspired criteria, such as the legitimacy of government expenditure, and that it uses these criteria as crucial elements for evaluating quality of policy. Hence, many scholars refer to this type of policy evaluation as 'judicial evaluation'.

During the post-war era, especially as a result of large-scale public investment programmes in the US, including on defence and space exploration, the need arose to scrutinize and evaluate government policy in a more economics-based way. The notion that perhaps government policy should be managed and evaluated in the same way as company policy gained ground, giving rise, during the 1960s and 1970s, to the concept of 'public management'. It was in the spirit of this era that the notion of policy evaluation as we know it today originated. Policy was expected to focus on solving problems, a train of thought which we have identified in section '1.2 Criteria for policy evaluation' as the rational-economic perspective on policy-making, an approach that prevailed during those years. From this point of view, policy evaluation would determine whether and to what extent the goals of a certain policy had been attained, whether those goals were actually attained through the policy intervention so that it could be said to be effective, and whether that policy was being pursued in the most appropriate or most efficient way. This approach led to the development and gradual sophistication of famous methods such as the Programme Planning and Budgeting System (PPBS), which were used for policy design and policy evaluation simultaneously. Apart from the policy domains characterized by huge public investments, such as defence and space exploration in the US, other policy fields that have been subjected to evaluative studies internationally are most often those of employment and education. In both cases, public authorities have a particular interest in the effectiveness of specific programmes targeting vulnerable or underprivileged categories. As will become apparent in Chapters 3 and 4, many methods of policy evaluation were created and developed specifically in those policy fields. Before that, Chapter 2 will consider some of the methodological problems that are typically associated with the evaluation of environmental policies.

With the advent of neo-liberalism and new public management during the 1980s and 1990s, (business) economics became even more important as the angle from which to evaluate public policy. Performance increasingly came to be seen as the key criterion. In fact, this was not just the case in policy evaluation, but also in policy development: the performance of government – or of the kind of autonomous administrative bodies that were increasingly entrusted with policy implementation – is gauged on the basis of indicators; the output to be generated is laid out in contracts; and subsidizing is made dependent upon the actual delivery of that output. Thus, again, part of the newly emerged business management monitoring systems and evaluation processes had been incorporated within policy development. This is why scholars refer to this type of evaluation either as 'administrative', alluding to its earlier stages, or as 'economic' or even 'managerial', with reference to its later and current stages.

During the course of the 1980s, however, other evolutions would unfold. In addition to effectiveness, the notion of legitimacy of government intervention increasingly came to the fore. Consequently, policy evaluation gradually came to apply such political evaluation criteria as legitimacy, acceptance, participation and responsiveness. In fact, analysing and evaluating the public support or legitimacy of policy almost developed into an independent field of research. Moreover, policy evaluation, because of its focus on public support and legitimacy, was increasingly shifting towards more participatory approaches. These approaches provided not only for the evaluation of the actual actors involved, but also for evaluation based on their objectives, wants and preferences with regard to content, as well as to the policy process and organization. It won't come as a surprise that this type of evaluation is most often referred to as 'political evaluation'. This type of evaluation is mostly carried out in close cooperation with policy-makers and other stakeholders in order to make policy evaluation as much a multi-actor activity as policy-making itself. Examples of participatory policy evaluation approaches are provided in Chapter 4.

As the latter set of criteria suggests, a gradual shift had taken place in the perspective adopted on policy evaluation: whereas policy evaluation was originally directed almost exclusively at administrative monitoring and economic accountability, it slowly also came to focus on aspects such as 'learning', reflection on the various policy mechanisms and generating responses to them that would improve policy, make it more effective, enhance its legitimacy, and so on. Over the last decades or so, 'learning' has become one of the buzzwords in organizational theory and in public policy studies, and some suggest learning to be the predominant contribution that policy evaluation can provide and/or should be aimed at. While we agree, in general terms, about the desirability of (organizational, social, governmental) learning, especially when facing very complex and uncertain environmental issues, one cannot consider 'learning' to be a more or less automatic (side) effect of policy evaluations. Even if evaluations are deliberately targeting learning, we know from literature on knowledge utilization, organizational change and institutional change that organizations and government bodies do differ substantially in their willingness and their capacity for learning. These characteristics, in turn, are related to features such as rigidity versus flexibility, openness for new information, and hierarchy versus horizontal styles of working, which are reported on indepth in policy studies. Policy evaluation, therefore, even though it comes up with high-quality research and with highly relevant recommendations, does not guarantee any learning. Nevertheless, some approaches in policy evaluation, particularly those emphasizing the importance of participation, also pay a great deal of attention to (increasing) the learning effect, as Chapter 4 will clarify in more detail.

1.2.2 The JEP triangle: The three rationalities of policy evaluated

Various policy scientists have pointed out that public policy is based on more than a single rationale or basic motive. Generally speaking, three underlying rationales of public policy are distinguished: a juridical or judicial rationale, an economic rationale (sometimes referred to as a business rationale) and a political rationale. Together these are known as the JEP triangle. Without presuming a one-to-one relation, these three rationales more or less reflect the three types of evaluation that we sketched above as they emerged throughout the history of policy evaluation. We will briefly elucidate each of these rationales because they also form the bases of three sets of criteria used for (environmental) policy evaluation.

The juridical or judicial rationale is related to the rule of law and to the principles of good governance. As stated above, the traditional criteria of policy evaluation by an audit office are in line with these criteria. The main issues of concern here are the protection of basic rights, the principles of lawfulness and the maintenance of law and order etc.: a set of basis principles and rulings that grew in number and international attention as time went on. These lay down a number of principles regulating the rules of play among public authorities (e.g. the principles of subsidiarity, policy hierarchy, multilevel governance, etc.) and between the public authorities and civil society (e.g. the principles of legal protection, etc).

In contrast, the economic or business rationale focuses mainly on policy goal attainment, effectiveness and efficiency. Economy, performance, enforceability, feasibility, etc. are all important focal points in this respect. Many of today's management tools for governance and its monitoring are in line with these criteria.

The political rationale behind policy refers to the principles at the core of democracy: representation; mandate and accountability; accessibility, openness and responsiveness; transparency and participation; etc. This rationale finds expression in various political rights and liberties, in the separation of powers (*trias politica*), in limitations on government power and so on, but also in the quest for legitimacy by policy-makers.

These three underlying rationales of policy are (even though their respective significance and importance may vary over time) invariably present in an ongoing political debate. At the same time, they help to distinguish three types of policy evaluation, as sketched above. And, more importantly for this section, these three rationales provide us with three sets of policy evaluation criteria. These criteria, clustered into typically juridical or judicial, managerial and political criteria, respectively, have given rise to the so-called JEP triangle (see Figure 1.2).

First and foremost, this figure demonstrates once again which criteria may be applied from each of the three perspectives. Of course, the criteria mentioned above and those described in Figure 1.2 need to be further 'operationalized' (i.e. they need to be expressed in terms of variables). Second, by juxtaposing the three sets of criteria in a triangle, it becomes clear that not only are the three rationales behind policy or the three clusters of policy evaluation criteria different, but they are also contradictory. The well-known dilemma of policy-makers, who must strike a balance between power and legitimacy, can now be translated in terms of the opposing criteria of economic efficiency, on the one hand, and political

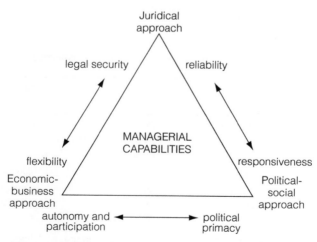

Figure 1.2 *The so-called juridical, economic and political criteria (JEP) triangle*

Source: Arts and Goverde (2006, p77), reproduced with permission of the authors and publisher

legitimacy, on the other. There is also an element of contradiction between the judicial criterion of legal security and the managerial criterion of flexibility. By highlighting these contradictions, the triangle also makes clear that any evaluation that takes into account only one perspective tends to be one sided. In other words, a balanced policy evaluation must encompass criteria from more than one perspective.

This, once again, suggests that an evaluation of effectiveness and efficiency should, in any case, be complemented with an assessment from other angles. Moreover, and coming back to the three perspectives set out in the previous section, Table 1.1 makes clear that 'effectiveness' may, indeed, have quite different meanings depending upon the perspective that one uses in policy evaluation.

Without further elaborating upon Figure 1.2 and Table 1.1, it is clear that an evaluation that focuses on managerial effectiveness and efficiency exclusively, however important these aspects may be, runs the risk of not shedding sufficient light on other evaluation criteria and other perspectives. It may, indeed, neglect certain qualities and inconveniences of the policy concerned and thus also ignore opportunities for learning and improving that particular policy.

1.2.3 Criteria of good governance?

For some time now, the United Nations has been promoting a number of principles of good governance – in this case, good public governance. The eight principles of good governance are rule of law; consensus-building; participation; responsiveness; transparency; accountability; equitability and inclusiveness; and effectiveness and efficiency (see Figure 1.3).

Table 1.1 *Effectiveness from three perspectives*

Perspective	Policy making is ...	Guiding metaphors	Success is ...
Rationalism	Problem-solving oriented	Policy cycle (regulatory cycle in engineering)	Problem-solving
Interaction	Interaction between agencies and interests involved	Networks, stakeholders, negotiation, deliberation	Network constitution, exchange and convergence
Institutionalism	Functioning of regimes; institutional arrangements	Path dependency versus institutional change (transition)	Institution-building; institutional (change) capacity

Figure 1.3 *The principles of good governance*

Source: UNESCAP (2008)

From an historical point of view, these eight principles may be understood to be the sum total of traditional judicial principles of appropriate governance, complemented by more recent managerial or economic, as well as political, principles. At the present juncture, these eight criteria constitute a kind of benchmark for good public governance. Their purpose, especially in a global context, is both to mobilize and to programme: they present states, their leaders and their citizens with an ideal in the hope that they will aspire to it. Additionally, these principles or criteria, which were already being used by critical non-governmental organizations (NGOs), are now also increasingly relied on by organizations such as the World Bank and the International Monetary Fund to evaluate the general quality of government and, thus, the credit worthiness of states. In this way, good governance has become a basic requirement for a country to be admitted to the international community. Of course, in this area, too, pragmatism sometimes trumps principle. The same holds for the notion of corporate governance: the management of mainly internationally operating companies is also increasingly evaluated on the basis of a multitude of criteria. Traditional evaluation criteria of business economics (important primarily to shareholders) have been complemented with aspects such as social entrepreneurship and sustainability (important primarily to stakeholders).

However, we are not concerned here with the actual application and impact of such principles. We simply want to demonstrate that the eight principles of good governance, frequently referred to in domains related to globalization, development, poverty, sustainability and environment, are, in fact, a temporary synthesis of decades, if not centuries, of policy evaluation and criteria development. Traditional legal criteria of lawfulness have been supplemented with recent political criteria such as participation, and with strongly managerially inspired criteria such as accountability. Contemporary policy evaluation will, in one way or another, need to strike a balance when applying these criteria. In Chapter 3 and 4 it will become apparent how various methods of policy evaluation take this into account.

REFERENCES

As already mentioned, a full reference list as is the case in most classical textbooks, is not provided here. For detailed references to the various methodological approaches, we refer to Chapters 3 and 4. What follows is a handful of books on policy evaluation that inspired us when preparing courses, when carrying out research in policy evaluation and when conceiving this book.

Arts, B. and Goverde, H. (2006) 'The governance capacity of (new) policy arrangements: A reflexive approach', in B. Arts and P. Leroy (eds) *Institutional Dynamics in Environmental Governance*, Springer, Dordrecht, The Netherlands
Bovens, M., t'Hart, P. and Peters, B.G. (eds) (2001) *Success and Failure in Public Governance: A Comparative Analysis*, Edward Elgar, Cheltenham, UK
Clarke, A. and Dawson, R. (1999) *Evaluation Research: An Introduction to Principles, Methods and Practice*, Sage, London
Dunn, W. N. (2003) *Public Policy Analysis: An Introduction*, 3rd edition, Prentice-Hall, Englewood Cliffs, NY
Edelenbos, J. and van Eeten, M. (2001) 'The missing link: Processing variation in dialogical evaluation', *Evaluation*, vol 7, no 2, pp204–210
EEA (European Environment Agency) (2001) *Reporting on Environmental Measures: Are We Being Effective?*, EEA, Copenhagen, Denmark
Fischer, F. (1995) *Evaluating Public Policy*, Nelson-Hall, Chicago, IL
Furubo, J. E., Rist, R. C. and Sandahl, R. (eds) (2002) *International Atlas of Evaluation*, Transaction Publishers, New Brunswick, NJ
Hage, M. and Leroy, P. (2007) *Stakeholder Participation Guidance for the Netherlands Environmental Assessment Agency: Main Document/Practice Guide/ Check List*, MNP/RU Nijmegen, www.mnp.nl/en/publications/2008/ StakeholderParticipation Guidance for theNetherlandsEnvironmental AssessmentAgency_MainDocument.html, accessed 1 March 2008
Hall, P. (1993) 'Policy paradigms, social learning and the state: The case of economic policy making in Britain', *Comparative Politics*, vol 25, no 3, pp275–296
Howlett, M. and Ramesh, M. (2003) *Studying Public Policy – Policy Cycles and Policy Subsystems*, Oxford University Press, Oxford, UK

Leeuw, F., Rist, R. C. and Sonnischen, R. C. (eds) (1994) *Can Governments Learn? Comparative Perspectives on Evaluation and Organisational Learning*, Transaction, New Brunswick, NJ

Madaus, G. F., Scriven, M. and Stufflebeam, D. L. (eds) (1986) *Evaluation Models: Viewpoints on Educational and Human Services Evaluation*, Kluwer-Nijhoff, Boston, MA

Owen, J. M. and Rogers, P. (1999) *Program Evaluation: Forms and Approaches*, Sage, London

Patton, M. Q. (1997) *Utilization-Focused Evaluation: The New Century Text*, Sage, Thousand Oaks, CA

Pressman, J. L. and Wildawsky, A. B. (1984) *Implementation: How Great Expectations in Washington Are Dashed in Oakland*, University of California Press, Berkeley, CA

Sabatier, P. A. and Jenkins-Smith, H. C. (eds) (1993) *Policy Change and Learning: An Advocacy Coalition Approach*, Westview Press, Boulder, CO

Stufflebeam, D. L. (2001) 'Evaluation models', *New Directions for Evaluation*, no 89

UNESCAP (United Nations Economic and Social Commission for Asia and the Pacific) (2008) 'What is good governance?', www.unescap.org/pdd/prs/projectactivities/ ongoing/gg/governance.asp, accessed 1 March 2008

Vedung, E. (2000) *Public Policy and Program Evaluation*, Transaction Publishers, New Brunswick, NJ

Worthen, B. R., Sanders, J. R. and Fitzpatrick, J. L. (1997) *Program Evaluation: Alternative Approaches and Practical Guidelines*, Longman Publishers, New York, NY

2

Problems and Limitations of Environmental Policy Evaluation

The previous chapter discussed various views on policy and policy evaluation, and provided an overview of criteria used in policy evaluation and how they have come about. While doing so we already touched upon a series of theoretical and conceptual (but also methodological) issues. Since this book does not go into theoretical debates, we restrict the discussion to methodological matters that seem inevitably linked to (environmental) policy evaluation. By doing so, we obviously do not intend to discourage the reader, but rather to provide a realistic picture of the problems encountered when conducting (environmental) policy evaluation, its possibilities and its limitations.

In the paragraph above, the word 'environmental' was twice placed between brackets when combined with 'policy evaluation' for a reason. Many of the methodological issues we intend to discuss are generic issues, inherent in policy evaluation, in general, irrespective of the policy domain. However, in this section we assume that some of these methodological issues are either fairly specific or more prevalent in the evaluation of environmental policy. This is where we place the emphasis.

In this chapter, we deal successively with problems and challenges relating to:

- the complexity of the policy field;
- the availability and collection of relevant data;
- elements such as time, scale and level of analysis;
- the question of causality and the choices required for cases; and
- the position of the evaluator and his or her findings, as well as the opportunity to have these findings used for policy change or at least for policy learning.

For each of these aspects, we highlight inherent problems in the context of policy evaluation, in general, and their particular relevance to environmental policy evaluation, as well as ways of dealing with them. The latter aspect will be addressed again in Chapters 3 and 4, when we describe the various policy evaluation methods and their actual or possible application to the environmental field, including empirical examples.

2.1 COMPLEXITY AND COMPLEXITY REDUCTION

As is the case with many policy fields, environmental policy is characterized by a large degree of complexity – in our case, the complexity of environmental problems, including the uncertainties related to it – or (in more epochal terms) by the interaction between mankind and the environment. Policy-makers and their advisers are often quick to reduce this complexity to a number of key variables. Complicated issues such as the loss of biodiversity, let alone climate change, are all too readily diminished to a series of variables and indicators, displayed in environmental assessment reports in single figures, and even further simplified into the widely used smileys (☺, ☺, ☹). It can be argued that such a radical reduction is the only feasible way of handling an issue, and of developing a meaningful policy and formulating workable policy measures.

BOX 2.1 THE QUALITY OF AIR IN URBAN AREAS: A HIGHLY COMPLEX ISSUE

A clear and topical example of complexity is the issue of air quality in urban areas. Air quality is determined by an extremely large number of factors. As far as the causes of pollution are concerned, there are elements such as production processes and mobility to take into account, all of which are, in turn, determined by economic and technological variables. The diffusion of, and the exposure to, air pollution relate to geophysical, meteorological, traffic, planning and housing factors, among others, which all may impact upon public health.

In this complex situation, a policy must be pursued to ensure that the quality of air in urban areas meets a number of (in this case, primarily European) standards. While the latter often reduce the problem to a pollutants threshold, it is clear that an adequate policy should go far beyond air quality standards solely, and should comprise a variety of factors, as mentioned above. Yet, even a good and coherent policy on air quality in urban areas cannot possibly cover all of these aspects and variables. Consequently, policy-makers resort to complexity reduction: they attribute a central role to certain variables and, subsequently, gear policy towards those variables, whether in a consistent and coherent fashion or not. In other words, they pursue a policy that tries to address part of the problem. Whether or not the aspect that is highlighted is the most crucial element is not always known in advance in complex situations. Moreover, issue reduction tends to 'average out' situations, and thus might overlook specific sources or neglect specifically vulnerable target groups, in this way missing the most urgent environmental or public health aspects.

Yet, the question rises as to whether such a reduction of an issue is valid and reliable, whether it is legitimate, or whether in one way or another the reduction implies a distortion of the nature of the problem itself. In the latter case, there is a risk that the ensuing policy measures may address another problem than they were originally intended to. This problem is generic in nature; but all those working in the environmental sphere are particularly sensitive to the possible biases that environmental indicators might entail. The issue is well documented and heavily disputed.

This issue of problem reduction is of particular interest here. It seems to us that any policy analysis and evaluation should pay sufficient attention to the question of how policy has dealt with the complexity of the issue at hand. And, of course, this question has to be followed by queries about *whom* or *what* played a decisive role in this regard. More importantly, still, is to know how the ensuing process of policy design and policy formulation unfolded (in terms of organization, instrumentation and implementation). After all, the subsequent evaluation will raise questions about the appropriateness of the chosen policy strategies and policy instruments, given the, albeit reduced, level of complexity.

From a (chrono)logical point of view, the question of how complexity reduction is undertaken and how appropriate the complexity reduction is will precede any evaluative questions about the policy's effectiveness and efficiency. It may, after all, be the case that a policy strategy is perfectly organized in terms of its instrumentation and implementation, and yet remains largely ineffective and inefficient because the original complexity has been incorrectly reduced.

In this context, a policy evaluation researcher may, in fact, choose one of two options. One option for the researcher is to take the complexity reduction for granted. In doing so, the researcher, in fact, adopts the reduction made by the policy-makers even though this is where the reason for policy failure may lie. In other words, the researcher adopts the policy goal as officially and formally set.

The other option is for the researcher to emphasize and analyse the complexity reduction, including all subsequent choices. Both approaches are encountered in practice. The choice between the two depends upon the assignment, the degree of freedom given by the client, and the relationship between the client and the researcher. We will return to the latter aspect in the last section of this chapter. In the chapters that follow, this issue will also be revisited, albeit in the context of the choice between what is often labelled as goal-based versus goal-free evaluation.

2.2 DATA AVAILABILITY AND DATA APPROPRIATENESS

Both policy-makers and policy researchers are often confronted with problems relating to the availability of data, also referred to as data scarcity, data incongruity and, in some cases, data overload. Encouraged by the Organisation for Economic

---

BOX 2.2 GOAL-BASED VERSUS GOAL-FREE

Like the *ex post* versus *ex ante* distinction, goal-based versus goal-free is a frequently used dichotomy when typifying policy evaluation research. And, as in the case of *ex post* and *ex ante*, this dichotomy is not entirely tenable.

If policy evaluation is goal-based, it takes as its starting point the policy goals that have been formally identified in laws, policy plans, etc. These formally set policy goals are not questioned, nor are the processes through which they have been determined. Clearly, then, what is being evaluated is the internal logic and outcome of policy. However, this at once implies that other criteria, such as the lawfulness of the policy goal, the legitimacy of the policy goal and (particularly in this section) the way in which it reduces complexity, cannot be applied.

Goal-free evaluation, on the other hand, gives the evaluator the freedom to evaluate exactly those items which he or she wishes to consider. This implies that the evaluator may also focus on the way in which policy goals have been set, as well as the appropriateness of those goals, including with regard to the complexity of the underlying problem.

Two remarks are in place in relation to the dichotomy. First, the distinction is not as sharp in practice as is suggested here. Almost all evaluations include evaluative conclusions of both types. Second, it is generally the client who ultimately decides between the two approaches. And, obviously, that client will not be inclined to have the goals challenged once they have been set (unless the client aims at criticizing the goals set by another competing government body).

There is another point to consider: these (political) circumstances of evaluation, along with theoretical and methodological issues, partly explain why policy evaluations, which are usually commissioned, tend to fit in with the 'policy-as-a-loop' approach rather than the 'policy-as-interaction' framework.

Co-operation and Development (OECD), the European Commission and the European Environment Agency in particular, European member states – as well as countries all over the world – encouraged, in turn, by the United Nations Environment Programme (UNEP) or other global institutions witnessed an enormous effort on environmental data collection and reporting over the last two decades or so. In particular, dedicated environmental assessment agencies contributed substantially to organize a more systematic, coherent, internationally comparable and scientifically sound way of data collection and data reporting. Both global institutions, such as the Intergovernmental Panel on Climate Change (IPCC), and domestic ones, and the gradually increasing interaction between these organizations, provided common formats for this environmental reporting. In some countries and at some international levels, data are even used as an asset to environmental policy evaluation.

Nevertheless, the problems of data scarcity, data incongruity and, as the case may be, data overload remain. We will briefly outline these three problems from a policy evaluation perspective. First and foremost, there are still areas where, despite the many efforts that have been made, data scarcity is a problem. While waste policy is a traditional and well-documented field of environmental policy-making, it can still be difficult, for example, to obtain reliable statistics on the amounts of certain types of waste, and the amount of waste that is reused through product or material recycling. Despite European and international definition effort, even the very definitions of waste vary, which causes huge problems in international comparative policy evaluation. The field of nature conservation policy, for example, displays substantially diverging forms of monitoring, resulting in data incongruity: data differ as a result of the collection methods used and the ways in which they are processed and analysed; consequently, data differ in their validity and reliability. There is more here than a mere methodological point: while nature conservation is a field in which data collection to a greater or lesser extent depends upon voluntary associations and non-governmental organizations (NGOs), other environmental policy fields, however, like waste and water, may largely rely on information gathering by private companies. Both ways of organizing the data collection and the data deliverance have their own risks of being biased.

In other cases, the problem is data overload: a sheer endless set of variables is available, all of which are potentially important. The selection of the most relevant data is an important or even crucial part of policy evaluation.

The above does not only hold for scientific data on the environment and nature, and on their causes and effects. Equally important in the context of policy evaluation is the availability of adequate data on the policy itself, and on how it is organized and implemented. This data may relate to budgets and manpower; to subsidizing and tax revenues; to the number of the Eco-Management and Audit Scheme (EMAS) or International Organization for Standardization (ISO) 140001 recognized companies; to the duration of certain steps in the policy process; to the participation of various groups in that process; to procedures in instrument choice; to procedural changes; to actual policy practices, and so forth. An adequate policy evaluation of the crucial processes in environmental policy, such as the determination and setting of environmental norms, and the granting of permits and policy enforcement, can only be achieved if organizational policy data are available. This, however, is not the case yet, partly because these processes and practices, and the day-to-day choices that they involve, have not been extensively documented and are not terribly transparent. Consequently, before proceeding with the evaluation of a policy, researchers may be required to collect such basic data themselves. But researchers may also conclude that, for reasons of unavailable and reliable data, a policy field cannot be evaluated. Evaluation is one of the issues addressed in Chapter 4.

Data availability and data quality sets one cluster of problems for both policy-making and policy evaluation, as already touched upon when referring to complexity reduction. The actual use that policy-makers make of data in itself,

Box 2.3 Climate change, complexity and uncertainty

Climate change, no doubt, is currently the best example of an area where data incongruity and data overload meet, and where, moreover, an insoluble complex issue presents itself. Since the climate issue was first reported and put on the agenda, an enormous amount of information, ranging from local to global data, has been collected relating to various phenomena. Moreover, these data originate in various disciplines. Despite this proliferation in available data, and despite the enormous work done by the IPCC in particular, no solution has been found to some of the uncertainties surrounding the issue. In fact, one could argue that uncertainty has increased in relation to certain aspects (e.g. the regionally differing impacts and costs of climate change, and mitigating and adaptive measures).

These uncertainties have been seized by some in order to encourage scepticism. This is not what we envisage, although it seems that with climate change we have reached the limits of human knowledge. And, yet, policy must be shaped and evaluated, 'anchoring amid uncertainty'. In this context, policy evaluation relates mainly to the question of how one should deal with uncertainty, how one should discuss it with stakeholders, and how to handle decision-making in spite of it.

The climate issue, the introduction of genetically modified organisms, the issue of small particulate air pollution, and other environmental issues are prime examples of complexity and uncertainty. However, the same intrinsic uncertainty manifests itself in relation to smaller-scale environmental questions, such as the presumed cancer-inducing effects of air pollution or the presumed health effects of long-term exposure to small doses of pollutants. Again, we notice that policy-makers resort (too) readily to reducing the (politically awkward) complexity that presents itself.

however, raises another number of interesting questions for policy evaluation. For example, on the basis of which data or indicators have the policy problem and goals been defined? Is a sufficient amount of data available on various aspects of the policy problem and goals, as well as with regard to the interests involved? Or do some aspects and parties have more data, and therefore more knowledge, at their disposal? Which assumptions and data have been relied upon when choosing certain policy instruments? Which data have been chosen for monitoring the policy during the implementation phase? Has one provided for an *ex post* evaluation? Certainly in the evaluation of policy effects and effectiveness, the availability of longitudinal data is essential.

Therefore, prior to research or in an early phase of the research process, clarity must be obtained about data availability and suitability. Throughout Chapters 3 and 4 it will become apparent that each method makes assumptions about data availability while, conversely, the relative unavailability of data will have inevitable methodological consequences. At any rate, if policy evaluation requires data collection, both money and manpower should be budgeted for.

Box 2.4 European Environment Agency critical of data availability

One of the most striking conclusions of broad and extensive research into policy effectiveness, conducted by the European Environment Agency (EEA), is that often a thorough evaluation simply cannot be carried out. One of the reasons is that the European Union (EU) and its member states pay (too) little attention to the fact that policy will, at some point, usually after its implementation, need to be evaluated. All kinds of data that are essential for such evaluations are hardly collected at all, let alone made available and accessible to third parties. The result is that the EEA is barely able to answer the basic question: 'Are we being effective?' (EEA, 2001).

Moreover, in various countries and at EU level, there is some controversy about who should provide and collect which data and who should evaluate on the basis of this data. Data are not a neutral product and, as this book further reports, environmental evaluation provokes further controversy about them.

In addition to the financial aspect, there is also the issue of sensitivity: information may be available but not accessible as it may be in the interest of the party under evaluation or, indeed, another party to restrict data access. Such sensitivities, which may be of a political, an internal-administrative or a commercial nature, must also be taken into account. Environmental policy evaluation already provoked controversies in different countries and at the European level. The quintessence of this controversy is similar: since the early 1970s, almost all countries have established ministries and other agencies for the design and the implementation of environmental policies. Environmental data gathering was an implicit and uncontroversial part of their mission and task until environmental agencies were set up, with the specific task of gathering environmental data and reporting on them. Some conceived this as a breakthrough in the assumed monopoly of data gathering by several agencies, while others regard environmental data as part of a country's common knowledge, available to all. Since the emergence of environmental policy evaluation, this first battle over competencies – in which well-established statistical information agencies also take part, at national as well as European level – has been complemented by a second one: policy evaluation tends to blur the pre-existing boundaries between agencies that were and are responsible for policy design and those held responsible for data collection only. One does not only witness a battle over competencies here. Simultaneously and, more generally, another issue at stake here is the (permanent construction of the) boundary between science and policy: some of the agencies involved stick to a scientific style on data gathering and reporting, while others rather refer to a more bureaucratic style.

2.3 TIMEFRAME, SPATIAL DIMENSION AND LEVEL OF ANALYSIS

The timeframe, the spatial dimension and the level of analysis are three essential aspects in (environmental) policy evaluation. Obviously, any decisions with regard to these elements should be taken jointly by the researcher and the client. In what follows, we outline some possibilities and limitations in this respect, and highlight some of the choices that need to be made.

2.3.1 Policy evaluation and time

For (environmental) policy evaluation, the time dimension is important in a number of ways. First and foremost, processes, especially in the environmental field, can unfold over occasionally very long periods. Effects, including those induced by policy, will only become visible in the distant future: this is the so-called *time lag effect*. In cases of groundwater protection or climate policy, we may be talking about a timeframe of dozens of years.

The time lag effect implies that, in a policy evaluation, an explicit choice needs to be made in relation to the relevant timeframe, considering that the output, outcome and eventual impact upon environmental quality can differ significantly. If a definitive effectiveness evaluation is out of the question, one will have to make do with (possibly repeated) interim evaluations of effects.

BOX 2.5 PROTECTION OF THE OZONE LAYER AND THE TIME LAG EFFECT

The 1985 Treaty of Vienna and the 1987 Montreal Protocol have been particularly effective in drastically reducing the production and consumption of ozone-depleting substances. Since the early 1990s, a 90 per cent reduction has been observed. Yet, according to the International Meteorological Organization, it will take at least 50 more years for the ozone layer to more or less recover; so, for the time being, a policy evaluation may be able to measure the policy output and the outcome in terms of both technological and behavioural changes (and in this sense it has scored well), while the actual environmental impact will only become measurable in the more distant future.

Second, the time dimension is significant to the policy itself. Policies rarely have a fixed beginning and end; usually new policies are piled upon old ones, or policy goalposts are shifted. If the latter has happened explicitly, then we need to consider why, on which basis and how. If the change of policy has been carried through silently or implicitly, then it is up to the researcher to make any amendments explicit. Politicians and policy-makers, in general, might tend either to explicitly flag a specific intervention as a policy shift or, conversely, deliberately emphasize the continuities in policy. Researchers should be sensitive to these rather political demarcations and historic boundary constructions in policy-making episodes.

In any case, the impact of a single policy measure is almost impossible to isolate from its context. And, yet, in policy evaluation, one often regards the introduction of a new plan or tool, a change of government, the end of a budget cycle or a similar milestone as the boundary of a policy period. A purposeful and explicit timeframe is necessary in order to arrive at a 'pure' policy evaluation.

2.3.2 Spatial dimension

Environmental issues are not bound by administrative borders. Problems such as air and water pollution, waste disposal, nature conservation and other environmental issues manifest themselves at different spatial scales. Yet, in policy evaluation and data collection, one usually only takes into account a single spatial dimension – namely, a national or sub-national administrative dimension. Likewise, state of the environment reports and similar environmental assessment reports tend to describe regional situations – partly for reasons of data availability – without worrying too much about any environmental damage that this region may be causing elsewhere in the world. The well-known 'ecological footprint' approach and its various elaborations attempt to take these effects into account; but for reasons of both data availability and (inevitable) methodological reductionism, the validity and reliability of these approaches are still restricted. Consequently, an environmental policy evaluation at national or sub-national level can paint a distorted picture.

Conversely, policy evaluation must, of course, apply to a relevant spatial scale. This implies that it should relate to a level where there is sufficient administrative capacity to resolve the issue at hand. But as environmental policies become more and more globalized, especially with regard to decision-making (e.g. the 1992 Earth Summit in Rio de Janeiro, the Kyoto Protocol and directives issued by the Intergovernmental Panel on Climate Change), strategies, instrumentation and implementation (e.g. joint implementation, emission trade, etc.), one can hardly point at one administrative level as the most appropriate for policy evaluation. As policies become more multilevel, so must evaluation, however great the methodological issues this raises.

2.3.3 Level of observation and analysis

This is an age-old pair of concepts in methodology, in general, and in policy evaluation methodology, in particular. In the latter case, the level of analysis refers to the administrative level at which one intends to analyse and evaluate policy-making. This may be at the global, continental (e.g. European) or any national or sub-national level of policy-making. The level of observation is the level at which a researcher collects the relevant empirical data. These two aforementioned levels do not necessarily coincide. An evaluation of the way in which a national government (level of analysis) supports its regional and local bodies of government in their environmental policies may, in fact, primarily use these lower levels of government as the level of observation. Likewise, an evaluation of the European Birds and Habitats Directive may be based on observations regarding local policies on nature reserves. Evaluations of this kind often focus on the domestic factors that further hinder the implementation of supranational measures (e.g. the way in which national differences persist or decrease due to international or European environmental policies).

The latter means that the evaluation takes seriously into account the multilevel character of policy, in which the interaction between the various levels is of central interest. In these cases, the 'operationalization' of the evaluation questions and the choice of an appropriate level of observation are very important, indeed. We have to admit, however, that although some excellent and fruitful evaluations of multilevel environmental policies have been carried out, there is not yet a standardized methodology for it.

2.4 CASE STUDIES AND LEVEL OF REPRESENTATION

The difference between the level of analysis and the level of observation is almost always of relevance to policy evaluations. After all, a policy evaluation does not encompass policy as a whole, but, rather, focuses on a subfield. However, we are mainly concerned here with the ample use that is made in policy evaluations of the case study method.

If the case history is approached quantitatively (e.g. by means of a sample for the purpose of a survey), one may claim representation, assuming that the methodological and statistical rules of sampling and analysis have been adhered to. However, such quantitative approaches have certain limitations. Moreover, they often measure the perception of environmental policy effects rather than the effects themselves, which is, for that matter, also an important source of knowledge in policy evaluation.

In many policy evaluations, as well as in the environmental field, one adopts a qualitative research design where one single or a few cases are studied. Usually, this does not result in a statistically representative picture of the overall issue. Yet, a qualitative approach is not necessarily weaker. If chosen carefully, even a small number of cases or a single case can be very revealing of the core issues in a policy field, the critical paths of some implementation processes, etc. A well-chosen single case study can succeed excellently in laying bare bottlenecks in policy-making, policy implementation and its actual effects, and may therefore result in a sound and valuable policy evaluation.

The selection of the case, again preferably in consultation with the body commissioning the study, is crucially important. There is sufficient methodological literature on how to choose a (single or a few) case(s), and on which arguments are decisive for their selection, given the aims of the research. Therefore, we restrict to the following: in the case of environmental policy evaluation that aims at learning, referred to earlier, and explicitly the goal of some of the methods discussed in chapter 3 and 4, it is recommended to choose a case with a high learning content. Further, and talking about learning, being able to conduct policy evaluation on the basis of separate cases over a number of years not only yields methodological experience; it also allows one to gradually evolve from an evaluation of separate policy measures to a more institutional evaluation of a broader policy field, and to evolve from a series of ex post studies to some ex ante endeavours.

2.5 THE IMPACT OF EVALUATIONS AND THE POSITION OF THE EVALUATOR

Policy evaluation may be fashionable today, even in the environmental field, but this is not to say that it is popular. After all, policy evaluation implies that policy-makers are made to look into a mirror. The image they see might not correspond with the one they have or wish to have of themselves. In sum, the findings of a policy evaluation frequently lead to debate or even to controversy. Actors concerned have different interpretations of the same 'facts' and, more importantly, some individuals might be sensitive towards 'interference' by science and policies, especially with regard to fear of political use or abuse of results. In order to maximize the impact of an evaluation report, we enumerate some important points here.

First, it is important to agree on whether the results, both in terms of conclusions and recommendations, would or should be published or otherwise made public. Some policy evaluations are intended exclusively for internal use. While this can be legitimate, certainly if the results are controversial, all parties should be prepared for leaks. Often, however, no prior agreements are made regarding public disclosure and publication (when, where, by whom, in what form, targeting which audience?). This shortcoming may, certainly in the case of unfavourable results, lead to debate. It is therefore important that these aspects be discussed explicitly and agreement reached upon it at the moment the assignment is granted. With regard to scientific evaluators, there is the additional complication that they are obliged to publish, so there must be clarity on which information can or cannot be disclosed. For that matter, even if publication is not an issue, it is important to reach agreement on the scope, tone and degree of precision of the forthcoming conclusions and recommendations.

Second, there is the follow-on effect of policy evaluations. Let us assume here that the request for policy evaluation has been made in good faith, and not for the purpose of undermining the ambitions of a competing administrative department, etc. Both the requester and the evaluator will then hold the hope that the results of the policy evaluation will have a subsequent impact upon policy. While this hope is justified, some realism is also in place here. There are several reasons for this. First, the result of a policy evaluation is just one of the factors affecting policy (re)formulation. Second, we know from research into knowledge utilization that knowledge, including scientific knowledge, is utilized very selectively in the (re)formulation of policy. As is the case with other parts of knowledge and information that are, or should be, used as input to policy-making, the intrinsic quality of that knowledge (in the case of evaluation: the quality of its conclusions and recommendations) is not the decisive factor here. Researchers thus could better give up their own rationalistic view on policy-making. Of much more importance than the intrinsic quality of the knowledge provided, is how these insights and recommendations fit into the political game. That 'fit' partly depends, as said earlier with regard to learning, upon the openness, flexibility, reflexivity and other characteristics of the commissioning organization and the opportunities that it offers to evaluators, but of course also upon similar characteristics in the policy domain as a whole. Although evaluators might wish to have an impact, they may find themselves on the outside, with their policy evaluation findings 'shelved' in the policy-making process: and there may be little they can do to prevent this from happening.

Both with regard to disclosure and follow-on effects, policy-makers and researchers should strike a balance between involvement and detachment, as is the case in any situation in which a researcher is required to make an expert judgement. Involvement can be conducive to more empathetic conclusions and recommendations, and to reticence with regard to publicly critical remarks. Distance, on the other hand, may lead to more objective conclusions and recommendations; but the likelihood that they will have an impact will be rather small. In any case, it is preferable that researchers and clients – and the 'object', if other than the client – should be frank about their mutual relationship and assess it regularly during the policy evaluation process.

Finally, approaches and methods of participatory policy evaluation, although they deliberately address the above mentioned issues, are no panacea for all of them. Yet, it is true that a participatory approach to (environmental) policy evaluation can, when adequately designed, enhance the researcher's involvement and insight, while allowing the 'object' to gain some understanding of the analysis and findings even during the evaluation process, so that they could already start to learn from and anticipate the results. This will enhance the perceived legitimacy of the process and the results on the part of the evaluated party, as well as other stakeholders, and will thus increase the likelihood of public disclosure and follow-on. This is partly why we give particular attention to some of these participatory (environmental) policy evaluation approaches in Chapter 4.

REFERENCES

This list of references is by no means exhaustive. Rather, we have gathered together some of the empirical research on environmental policies that address the problems and issues dealt with in this chapter (e.g. the effectiveness and causality issue, the multi-actor and multi-level features, question about time lags, etc.) and that have been an inspiration to us.

Becerra, S. (2003) *Protéger la Nature – Politiques Publiques et Régulations Locales en Espagne et en France*, PhD thesis, Université de Toulouse, Le Mirail, Toulouse, France

EEA (European Environment Agency) (2001) *Reporting on Environmental Measures: Are We Being Effective?*, EEA, Copenhagen, Denmark

Haverland, M. (1998) *National Autonomy, European Integration and the Politics of Packaging Waste*, Thela Thesis Publishers, Utrecht, The Netherlands

Hilden, M., Lepola, J., Mickwitz, P., Mulders, A., Palosaari, M., Similä, J., Sjöblom, S. and Vedung, E. (2002) *Evaluation of Environmental Policy Instruments: A Case Study of the Finnish Pulp and Paper and Chemical Industries*, Monographs of the Boreal Environment Research no 21, pp9–11

Scriven, M. (1991) 'Pros and cons about goal-free evaluation', *American Journal of Evaluation*, vol 12, no 1, pp55–62

Skou Andersen, M., Lerche, D., Kristensen, P. and Smith, C. (2005) *Effectiveness of Urban Wastewater Treatment Policies in Selected Countries: An EEA Pilot Study*, European Environment Agency, Copenhagen, Denmark

Skovgaard, M., Jacobsen, H., Vrgoc, M. and Feehan, J. (2005) *Effectiveness of Packaging Waste Management Systems in Selected Countries: An EEA Pilot Study*, European Environment Agency, Copenhagen, Denmark

Van Der Meer, F. B. and Edelenbos, J. (2006) 'Co-operation evaluation in multi-actor policy processes: Accountability, learning and co-operation', *Evaluation*, vol 12, no 2, pp201–218

Van der Zouwen, M. (2006) *Nature Policy Between Trends and Traditions – Dynamics in Nature Policy Arrangements in the Yorkshire Dales, Doñana and the Veluwe*, Eburon Publishers, Nijmegen/Delft, The Netherlands

3

Approaches to (Environmental) Policy Evaluation

Chapter 1 introduced the main concepts in policy studies insofar as they are relevant to policy evaluation. Moreover, it outlined three possible perspectives on policy and, hence, on policy evaluation. Even though introductory, it should be clear from those pages that there are divergent theoretical positions on, and ensuing methodological approaches to, policy evaluation. 'Effectiveness' or 'success', it would appear, are not the only evaluation criteria. As a matter of fact, these notions are, to say the very least, not univocally defined.

Over the years, the divergent theoretical positions on, and methodological approaches to, policy evaluation have led to the design, elaboration and testing of a series of methods for answering policy evaluation questions. While we will not emphasize the differences between these approaches, the reader will easily recognize the divergent conceptions of 'policy' and the various methodological starting points applied.

Again, the list of approaches presented here is by no means exhaustive. As stated in the 'Introduction' to this book, we have selected those approaches which, to our knowledge and in our experience, are most appropriate in the context of particular evaluative questions in the environmental field. That is also why each of the presentations begins with a number of queries and questions that we picked up from evaluative practice. These real life questions may help the reader of this book to identify the most suitable methods for his or her purpose.

The approaches are presented in a systematic way. For each method, we provide three crucial blocks of information. First, we elucidate the basic characteristics, assumptions and goals of the approach under the heading 'Elucidation and context'. Next, we explain which steps need to be taken in applying the approach, under the heading 'Methodology'. Finally, we provide bibliographical references in order to give the reader access to additional information on the approach concerned. In the 'References' section at the end of the chapter, we also pay particular attention to empirical examples of how the approach or method has been applied in the environmental field or, if unavailable, in an adjacent field of policy-making. These examples will provide more concrete insight into the peculiarities of the environmental field as discussed in Chapter 2.

Each of these three main aspects is analysed in further detail. Box 3.1 summarizes the explanatory format applied to each of the approaches.

In this chapter, the content is structured as follows:

1 needs analysis;
2 programme theory evaluation;
3 case study evaluation;
4 experiment and quasi-experiment;
5 formative/developmental evaluation;
6 goal-free evaluation;
7 impact assessment:
   • social impact assessment;
   • environmental impact assessment;
   • regulatory impact assessment;
8 cost-benefit analysis and cost-effectiveness analysis;
9 logframe method;
10 multi-criteria analysis;
11 realistic evaluation.

BOX 3.1 EXPLANATORY FRAMEWORK FOR THE METHODS IN POLICY EVALUATION

Elucidation and context

• The essence of the method:
   – What?
   – When?
   – Advantages and disadvantages?
• Historical context.
• Position in research and evaluation context.

Methodology

• Steps in the application of the method.
• Remarks.

References

• Primary and additional references.
• Examples.

Finally, we should point out that, in this chapter, we focus on approaches to answering evaluation questions in the strict sense (i.e. evaluation approaches based upon one or several of the criteria introduced in Chapter 1). Then, in Chapter 4, we consider approaches that provide answers to questions about the design of evaluation research, such as how can I assess the evaluability of a policy (sub-)field? What are the advantages and risks of participatory evaluation?

3.1 NEEDS ANALYSIS

Exemplary evaluation question relating to needs analysis

- Do the policy objectives as policy-makers have set them address actual policy needs?

3.1.1 Elucidation and context

The essence of the method

What?

Although the method is referred to as needs analysis, it is actually an evaluation method. Needs analysis asks critical questions about the needs that policy tries to satisfy. By confronting policy and its results or expected outcomes with policy needs, the evaluator assesses policy for its relevance.

When?

Needs analysis is concerned with the first phase in the policy cycle: policy formation or the determination of policy goals. The results of a needs analysis may be used to make adjustments to policy. Consequently, the evaluation should take place at a moment when policy adjustment to relevant needs is still possible.

Advantages and disadvantages?

The main advantage of needs analysis is that the evaluation focuses on the reasons for a policy. By assessing policy in the light of society's policy requirements, one gains insight into the relevance of that policy. The main disadvantage is that weighing up various policy needs and requirements is a politically sensitive matter and, in many cases, will inevitably lead to criticism of the evaluation outcome.

Historical context

Needs analysis is regarded as an important component of programme evaluation. In the US, programme evaluation has become synonymous with policy evaluation. Although a (policy) programme is not the same as a policy (policy is more encompassing), we can safely say that programme evaluation represents an important direction in the methodological literature on policy evaluation.

The origins of the programme evaluation approach lie in the field of social policy evaluation. In particular, the programmes enacted under the so-called Great Society policy of US presidents John F. Kennedy and Lyndon B. Johnson worked as catalysts for the emergence and development of programme evaluation. Many of these Great Society programmes had been ill prepared and would therefore prove unsuccessful and ineffective. This, in turn, gave rise to a need for a kind of evaluation that would ultimately lead to better programmes.

Although the tradition of programme evaluation lies primarily within the field of social policy, the approach can be applied in any social policy area concerned with organized social action, including environmental policy.

Research and evaluation context

Programme evaluation is therefore an evaluation tradition rather than an evaluation method. In fact, five evaluation methods fit into this tradition (see Box 3.2).

Box 3.2 THE FIVE METHODS OF PROGRAMME EVALUATION

1 Needs analysis.
2 Programme theory analysis (see Section 3.2 'Programme theory evaluation').
3 Policy process analysis.
4 Impact analysis (see Section 3.7 'Impact assessments').
5 Efficiency analysis (see Section 3.8 'Cost-effectiveness analysis (CEA) and cost-benefit analysis (CBA)').

Owen and Rogers (1999) regard needs analysis as a form of proactive evaluation. In other words, they consider it to be part of an evaluation approach where policy is adjusted prior to implementation.

3.1.2 Methodology

Steps in needs analysis

Needs analysis encompasses five steps (Rossi et al, 2004):
We will briefly discuss each of these steps.

Box 3.3 THE FIVE STEPS OF NEEDS ANALYSIS

1 Description of the problem.
2 Determination of the scope of the problem.
3 Identification of the target group.
4 Description of the target group.
5 Description of the required policy.

Description of the problem
Together with step 2, this initial step will provide insight into the issue at hand. The starting point for the problem definition is stakeholder dissatisfaction. This dissatisfaction may manifest itself as a need, a want or a desire. Depending upon how the dissatisfaction is assessed, the evaluator may draw conclusions with regard to the severity of the problem. Since a problem is defined as a social construct that is the product of the viewpoints of a variety of actors (see also Section 4.4 'Constructivist evaluation'), it is difficult to assess objectively. The perception problem is subsequently translated into a policy problem. In practice, the description of the problem usually boils down to a critical exploration of the political appraisal of the issue at hand. We should stress the significance of the term 'critical' here. It is crucially important in avoiding errors as the problem experienced by the stakeholders is translated into a political (and, ultimately, a policy) problem. In sum, we may say that the evaluator describes the problem on the basis of the stakeholders' perceptions of it.

Determining the scope of the problem
In this phase we try to answer questions of when, where and how big:

- *When?* When does the problem occur? Is there a beginning and an end?
- *Where?* Where does the problem occur? How extensive is this area? What are its geographical boundaries?
- *How big?* What is the scope of the problem?

By answering these three questions, one obtains a problem outline. Only if the scope of the problem is known can one assess whether the policy response is proportional to the problem. This part of needs analysis is complex as it depends first and foremost on quantitative data, which are often scarce, incomplete and thus not representative (see Chapter 2). In this step of the methodology, we rely on existing data and indicators.

In addition, we incorporate relevant descriptive elements, such as contextual information, within the analysis. To this end, we use data from organizations, surveys and interviews of privileged witnesses. In the primary references for this section provided at the end of the chapter, little or no attention is paid to interviewing. However, it is our firm belief that, especially in relation to environmental policy, relying on privileged witnesses is a very valuable research approach.

Determination of the target group
In order to assess whether policy is adequately geared to the needs of the target group, one obviously should know who belongs to that target group. The target group may be an individual, an organization, an enterprise, a population

group or even a physical entity (e.g. a water treatment installation or a waste incinerator).

We distinguish between direct and indirect target groups:

- By direct target groups we mean those who are assumed to feel the immediate effects of the policy measure. For example, in household waste policy, the direct target group is the population who wants household refuse to be processed.
- The indirect target group is made up of those individuals whose needs policy-makers wish to meet in the second instance. In the example above, the indirect target group consists of the group of local authorities who play a part in household waste policy.

Description of the target group

Once the target group has been determined, the evaluator can draw up its profile. The information contained in this description enables the evaluator to make a better assessment of the extent to which problem and policy responses are geared to one another. Often in needs analysis, when drawing up the target group profile, a distinction is made between three categories: target group with a risk, target group with a need and target group with a demand for something. The difference between these three categories lies in the importance of the need. A target group facing a risk has a need for that risk to be reduced or eliminated. A target group with a need is characterized by an interest in being served by policy. A target group who demands something is characterized by the fact that the absence of the desired item is central.

Description of required policy

In this step, the analyses made in the foregoing steps are brought together. This synthesis will enable one to answer the question: what is the problem and what is the most appropriate policy (response)? In this context, one needs to pay attention to the specific characteristics of both the problem and the policy. Once this question has been answered, the next step is to compare with policy practice: is the current policy response optimally geared to existing needs? The answer to that question implies an evaluation of policy.

Remarks

Besides the primarily quantitative approach taken in this method, there are a number of qualitative alternatives. The primary reference, for example, mentions the use of focus groups and informants. Berkowitz, in Reviere et al (1996), adds to this the option of surveys, and emphasizes the role of mixed methods (see Section 4.9 'Mixed-method evaluation').

References and Examples

Primary and additional references

Owen, J. and Rogers, P. (1999) *Program Evaluation: Forms and Approaches*, Sage, London

Posavac, E. and Carey, R. (2003) *Program Evaluation: Methods and Case Studies*, Prentice Hall, Upper Saddle River, NJ

Reviere, R. (ed) (1996) *Needs Assessment: A Creative and Practical Guide for Social Scientists*, Taylor and Francis, Washington, DC

Rossi, P., Lipsey, M. W. and Freeman, H. E. (2004) *Evaluation. A Systemic Approach*, Sage, Thousand Oaks, CA

Shadish, W. R., Cook, T. D. and Leviton, L. C. (1991) *Foundations of Program Evaluation*, Sage, Newbury Park, CA

Wholey, J. S., Hatry, H. P. and Newcomer, K. E. (2004) *Handbook of Practical Program Evaluation*, Wiley and Sons, San Francisco, CA

Examples

McDuff, M. (2002) 'Needs assessment for participatory evaluation of environmental education programs', *Applied Environmental Education and Communication*, no 1, pp25–36

This article reports on the application of needs analysis in a participatory evaluation study of the Wild Life Clubs of Kenya, a grassroots wildlife conservation organization. In this case, analysis of the evaluation needs led to an evaluation model in which participation is central.

Mahon, J. R. and Miller, R. W. (2003) 'Identifying high-value greenspace prior to land development', *Journal of Arboriculture*, vol 29, no 1, pp25–33

This article deals with land development, in which (according to the authors) ecologic, social and economic benefits of community greenspace are often overlooked. The authors provide a methodology for locating high-valued greenspace using Stevens Point, Wisconsin, US, as a case study. In order to evaluate selection criteria for parcels, a needs analysis is made based on existing data sources. The ecological, recreational and aesthetic value of parcels proved to be most important.

3.2 PROGRAMME THEORY EVALUATION

Exemplary evaluation questions relating to programme theory evaluation

- To what extent do policies help to attain the goals set?
- Do the goals that policy-makers have set correspond with existing policy needs?
- Are the available policy tools suitable for attaining the goals set?
- What are the expected (side) effects of policy? How should we assess these effects?

3.2.1 Elucidation and context

The essence of the method

What?

Programme theory evaluation (PTE) comes in various forms. Rogers et al (2000, p5) describe PTE as follows: PTE 'consists of an explicit theory or model of how the programme causes the intended or observed outcomes and an evaluation that is at least partly guided by this model'. In other words, it involves the development of an explanatory model that is used as a basis for policy evaluation.

PTE is an evaluation method in which programme theory is central. The programme theory consists of the assumptions and rationales upon which policy is based. It encompasses the beliefs and expectations of policy-makers with regard to the course of policy. In PTE, an assessment is made of the quality of the underlying assumptions of policy. One also ascertains whether the policy needs, goals and tools, and the (presumed) outcomes, connect in a logical manner.

Some scholars distinguish a second variant of PTE: policy theory evaluation. The purpose of this second variant of PTE is for the evaluator to be able to make statements about causal relationships between the policy intervention and the (presumed) policy effects. This approach also allows one to draw conclusions with regard to the contribution of policy to the policy outcome attained.

When?

The first variant of PTE (evaluation of the programme theory) can be used either *ex ante* or *ex post*. The quality of the programme theory can be assessed either before policy is implemented or after.

The second variant of PTE (policy theory evaluation) is applied in an *ex post* setting. In order to assess the causal relationship between the policy intervention and the presumed policy outcome, one first needs to implement the programme: one has to be able to measure the effects.

Advantages and disadvantages?

PTE offers a number of advantages:

- PTE leads to statements regarding, among other things, the causal relationship between policy and the presumed policy effects without quantitative research.
- In situations where the available means for research are limited, PTE can be a worthwhile alternative. PTE yields useful information without excessive deployment of financial resources or personnel.
- PTE is combinable with other methods. It is, for example, applied in realistic evaluation (see Section 3.11 'Realistic evaluation') and evaluability assessment (see Section 4.7 'Evaluability assessment').

The main disadvantage of PTE is that it makes use of little or no quantitative empirical evidence. This lack of 'hard evidence' for the relations between the various elements of PTE undermines the credibility of research results obtained in this way.

Historical context

During the 1960s, Suchman (1973) argued that research into the 'chain of policy objectives' was a valuable approach to policy evaluation. In this context, he focused on three elements:

1   the policy programme;
2   the policy objectives; and
3   possible intervening processes.

In the 1970s, scholars such as Weiss (1973, 1977) carried out evaluation research on the basis of so-called causal models. In subsequent years, PTE was used with increasing frequency as an evaluation method. However, the real breakthrough came towards the end of the 1980s, with two influential contributions by Bickman (1987) and Wholey (1987), published in the journal, *New Directions for Evaluation*. Both authors used the notion of programme theory for evaluation purposes.

Research and evaluation context

Most clients of evaluations, particularly in the Anglo-Saxon world, tend to demand a form of PTE. This, in part, explains why most books on policy evaluation contain a chapter on PTE (Madaus et al, 1983; Rossi et al, 1999).

Earlier, the field of application of PTE had consisted mainly in education policy and social policy simply because these are the two policy areas with the richest tradition in evaluation. However, PTE can, in principle at least, also be applied in any other policy domain.

3.2.2 Methodology

Steps in programme theory evaluation

Two steps are distinguished:

1 outlining of the programme theory;
2 use of the programme theory for policy evaluation.

Outlining the programme theory

There are three approaches to outlining a programme theory:

1 *The deductive approach.* In this approach, the programme theory is outlined after analyses of programme theories previously developed by academics.
2 *The inductive approach.* The inductive approach starts with fieldwork: interviews, observation of policy-making, document analysis, etc. This fieldwork yields data and insights. These elements are the building blocks upon which the programme theory is developed.
3 *The user-focused approach.* In this approach, the perception of the policy 'users' takes centre stage. In other words, one starts from the theory of the user. Outlining the programme theory in this way is very much a group process.

Leading evaluators such as Pawson and Tilley (2003) (see also Section 3.11 'Realistic evaluation') recommend a combination of the three above approaches.

Van de Graaf and Hoppe (2000) put forward a number of principal rules for developing a programme theory. These rules are, in fact, six substeps:

1 Collect as many documents as possible on the policy in question.
2 Reconstruct the goal tree of the policy in question. The goal tree represents the various policy objectives, which are related to each other. Each goal or objective indicates which situation is aimed at and which actions are required to attain that situation.
3 Identify causal and final arguments on means-and-goals relationships of policy. In this substep, the evaluator tries to indicate the causal relationship between the resources deployed and the policy effects.
4 Identify normative arguments for the means and goals of the policy. This substep is not so different from the previous one. Van de Graaf and Hoppe (2000) distinguish between causal–final and normative arguments. Consequently, they divide the identification of programme relationships into different substeps. For substeps 3 and 4, they compile two series of questions that provide the evaluator with a structure for identifying the different arguments.
5 Design a model-based synthesis of the results of steps 3 and 4. This yields the programme theory.

6   Introduce estimated probabilities and amounts into the model. In this step, the model is further refined on the basis of the policy-maker's assessment of the likelihood that a certain effect will occur. In addition, the scope of the effects as estimated by the policy-maker is incorporated by adding information on effect amounts.

Application of programme theory in policy evaluation

Although there are various ways of applying programme theory in policy evaluation, we may broadly distinguish between two groups of applications:

1   The first group uses the programme theory to ascertain which policy elements generate which effects. Especially in the case of large-scale evaluations, this approach is often chosen. One of the main benefits of such an evaluation is that, in the case of suboptimal goal attainment, it allows the policy evaluator to discriminate between failure of the programme theory and implementation deficits. By evaluating the programme theory, the evaluator is able to make statements regarding possible explanatory factors for the suboptimal goal attainment. This way, the evaluator is able to distinguish between an ill-considered policy and a badly implemented policy. This approach ties in with policy theory evaluation.
2   The second group uses programme theory for less ambitious purposes (i.e. to make limited adjustments to (the organization of) policy). This approach is taken mostly in more modest evaluations and does not strive to gain insight into the causal relationships between the policy intervention and (presumed policy) effects. Even though this approach is less ambitious, it is still valuable because it can provide useful information about the performance of an organization. This method is aligned with the 'evaluation of the programme theory' variant.

Remarks

While policy-makers are often positively inclined towards drawing up a programme theory, they are usually not so readily prepared to compare the programme theory with policy in practice. This is down to the rather confrontational nature of PTE. It is, after all, not pleasant as a policy-maker to have to discover with hindsight that the assumptions you made were erroneous.

Importantly, in the application of PTE, one needs to make sure that the evaluator does not lose himself/herself in theoretical considerations about the quality of the programme theory. Sights should be firmly set on resolving the societal issue that lies at the heart of the policy, not on optimizing the quality of programme theory.

References and Examples

Primary and addtional references

Bickman, L. (1987) 'The functions of program theory', *New Directions for Evaluation*, no 33, pp5–18

Leeuw, F. L. (2003) 'Reconstructing program theories: Methods available and problems to be solved', *American Journal of Evaluation*, vol 24, no 1, pp5–20

Madaus, G., Scriven, M. and Stufflebeam, D. L. (1983) *Evaluation Models*, Kluwer-Nijhoff, Boston, MA

Rogers, P., Petrosino, A., Huebner, T. and Hacsi, T. (2000) 'Program theory evaluation: Practice, promise, and problems', *New Directions for Evaluation*, no 87

Rossi, P. H., Lipsey, M. W. and Freeman, H. E. (2004) *Evaluation: A Systematic Approach*, Sage, Thousand Oaks, CA

Stame, N. (2004) 'Theory-based evaluation and types of complexity', *Evaluation*, vol 10, no 1, pp58–76

Suchman, E. A. (1973) *Evaluative Research: Principles and Practice in Public Service and Social Action Programs*, Russel Sage Foundation, New York, NY

Van de Graaf, H. and Hoppe, R. (2000) *Beleid en politiek: Een inleiding tot de beleidswetenschap en de beleidskunde*, Coutinho, Bussum, The Netherlands

Weiss, C. H. (1972) *Evaluation Research: Methods for Assessing Program Effectiveness*, Prentice Hall, Englewood Cliffs, NY

Weiss, C. H. (ed) (1977) *Using Social Research in Public Policy Making*, Heath, Lexington, MA

Wholey, J. S. (1987) 'Evaluability assessment: Developing program theory', *New Directions for Evaluation*, no 33, pp77–92

Examples

Shipley, R. (2002) 'Visioning in planning: Is the practice based on sound theory?', *Environment and Planning A*, vol 34, no 1, pp7–22

This article examines the use of 'visioning' in planning processes (creating images of the future to serve as goals or guides for planning decisions). The author indicates that visioning became closely linked to public participation, and that many consultants and municipal planners have used it. However, there has been little or no examination of the theoretical underpinnings of the practice. This study examines various data sources to articulate the underlying assumptions or theory-like statements about visioning. The resulting analysis shows that there are also profound weaknesses in parts of the underlying theory.

Lindgren, L. (2001) 'The non-profit sector meets the performance-management movement: A programme-theory approach', *Evaluation*, vol 7, no 3, pp285–303

In Sweden, popular adult education (PAE) is a field of public policy in which the non-profit sector takes up an important role. Since the introduction of *managerialism*, the Swedish government obliges the non-profit sector to take performance measures as evidence of accountability and results. In this article, the author employs a programme theory approach to uncover that some performance measures in Swedish PAE are, in fact, contradictory to the motives underlying the Swedish government's support to PAE. Folk high schools and study associations are forced to 'meet the numbers' (i.e. numbers that only, to a minor extent, are consistent with the PAE's programme theory).

3.3 CASE STUDY EVALUATION: CASE STUDY RESEARCH

Exemplary evaluation questions relating to case study research

- Which policy should be selected from a set of alternatives? Which policy alternative is the most desirable, feasible and affordable?
- Why does policy (fail to) achieve its goals?
- Can we, from a particular and well-chosen case (or cases), identify a causal relationship between the policy intervention and the effect achieved?

3.3.1 Elucidation and context

The essence of the method

What?

Case study evaluation (CSE) is, first and foremost, a general research method. However, it can also be applied for evaluation purposes, as Yin (2003a), in particular, advocates. Yin (2003a, p13) defines CSE as 'an empirical enquiry that investigates a contemporary phenomenon within its real-life context'.

More specifically, CSE is a method for studying and evaluating government interventions in their specific settings. According to Yin (2003a, p5), CSE explains how and why a certain policy has worked. By scrutinizing policy, within the confines of a case, the evaluator acquires insight into how policy is functioning and why. On the basis of these findings, the evaluator can then assess policy.

Yin (2003a) distinguishes between two variants of CSE, depending upon whether it involves single or multiple case studies. Patton (2002) refers to 'nested' and 'layered' case studies. A 'nested' case study is a single case within its context. A layered case study consists of various smaller case studies, all of which yield information for answering the evaluation. In this context, Yin (2003a) refers to embedded and holistic cases. Neither Patton nor Yin's distinction is concerned with the number of cases, but with the number of units of analysis. A nested or embedded case study encompasses one unit of analysis, while a layered or holistic case study encompasses several units of analysis.

When?

CSE is a research method that can be applied in any phase of the policy cycle, as mentioned in Chapter 1. It is appropriate for analysing and assessing agenda-setting, policy formation, policy choices and policy implementation. The most important criterion for determining whether a case study evaluation is desirable is the nature of the research question. If the evaluation question concerns an explanation (qualitative understanding), then a case study is a valid option. Likewise, CSE may be applied to weigh up different policy alternatives, provided that a case is available for each of the alternatives.

Advantages and disadvantages?

Case study evaluation offers a number of advantages:

- CSE assesses policy and how it relates to its context. This yields added value in situations where it is unclear where a policy ends and the policy context begins. After CSE, one should be able to define the boundary between the two more sharply.
- CSE provides for in-depth research: if the method is applied adequately, it will offer insight into the underlying mechanism of the policy under evaluation.
- Case studies tend to tie in closely with the environment of the users of the evaluation report. A CSE report is usually accessible because of the familiarity of the descriptions of policy practice.

There is, however, also a significant disadvantage. The results of case studies are not particularly robust. Any conclusions drawn are restricted to the case under scrutiny.

Historical context

Case study evaluation originated during the 1980s. The method developed out of interest in the so-called plausible rival hypotheses theory on the functioning of policy.

Plausible rival hypotheses can be approached either from the randomization paradigm or from the isolation paradigm. While the former tries to eliminate external influences through randomization, the latter isolates such external influences and studies them. Particularly in experiments, we notice the impact of the randomization paradigm: individuals are randomly allocated to either the experimental or the control group. This randomness would suggest that the resulting groups are comparable. In the case of the isolation paradigm, matching is applied. As a result, the chance factor, which is inherent in randomized allocation, is eliminated. Individuals are allocated to the experiment groups on the basis of a number of characteristics. This way, the evaluator is able to compose various comparable groups.

Case study evaluation fits into the second approach (i.e. the isolation paradigm). Historically speaking, CSE, together with quasi-experiments, emerged in response to the once predominant experimentation method.

Stake, in Madaus et al (1986, p284), assesses the future of CSE positively: 'Case studies are likely to continue to be popular because of their style and to be useful for exploration for those who search for explanatory laws.'

Research and evaluation context

Yin (2003a) compares case studies with experiments, archival research and trend analysis. According to him, a case study is the only method which, in a situation where one has no control over the context, allows one to answer the questions of how and why in relation to policy.

Swanborn asserts that it is self-evident that experimentation plays a central role in healthcare, that case studies are used mainly in public administration, and that quasi-experiments are most suitable for studying education (classroom settings) (Swanborn, 1999, p29). This indicates that Swanborn, like Yin, considers CSE as the method *par excellence* for public administration science and evaluations.

3.3.2 Methodology

Steps in a case study evaluation

Prior to a case study evaluation, one needs to decide whether to go with a single or a multiple case study. Multiple case studies are preferable as they yield more reliable evaluation results. However, in the following situations, a single case study is also a viable option:

- if a theory needs to be tested;
- if a unique case needs to be studied/evaluated (i.e. in a situation where there are no comparable cases);
- if that single case is a representative case;
- if the evaluation pertains to a pilot project (i.e. no precedent);
- as the first step in a longitudinal evaluation.

After deciding on a multiple or a single case study approach, the following steps are taken as outlined in Box 3.4.

BOX 3.4 THE FOUR STEPS IN A CASE STUDY EVALUATION

1 Design the case study.
2 Collect the data.
3 Analyse data collected.
4 Report on findings.

Design of the case study

The design phase of a case study evaluation consists of five components:

1 *Description of the research object.* This may be an actor, a policy, an event or an organization.
2 *The research questions.* As we have seen, these are 'how' and 'why' questions relating to the research object. Other questions, including quantitative ones (how much, how long) may also be answered within the framework of a case study. However, the emphasis lies on the 'how' and 'why' questions.
3 *The evaluation hypotheses.* When formulating the hypotheses, the evaluator makes explicit certain expectations with regard to the answers to the research questions.
4 *The evaluation hypotheses should strive for a logical link with research findings.* This can be achieved in various ways. A common approach is pattern matching, where two hypotheses are tested against empirical evidence. Hypothesis 1 is an effect hypothesis, or an assumption about what will happen when policy is implemented; hypothesis 2 is a no effect hypothesis, or an assumption about what will happen when policy is not implemented. Both hypotheses presuppose a certain pattern, by which we mean a series of interconnected events. These patterns are confronted with the pattern as if emerges from empirical observation. The hypothesis with the pattern that corresponds most closely to the empirical pattern is subsequently regarded as more reliable than the other hypothesis. This component, together with the fifth (i.e. evaluation criteria), has been least developed by Yin (2003a).
5 *The evaluation criteria.* Assessing the relationship between the data and the hypotheses (policy evaluation) is simple if one observes strongly diverging trends or patterns.

Data collection

In this context, the following focal points are important:

• First and foremost, the person conducting the case study should be a highly trained and experienced researcher. Observation and interviewing, especially in the context of a case study, require skills that are only acquired after years of practical experience.
• Preparation of the fieldwork and a literature study should be thoroughly conducted. For this purpose, one needs to deploy several researchers and develop a clear protocol.
• A pilot case study is highly recommended. This will enable the researcher to detect and remedy any shortcomings in the data collection strategy.

In the data collection activity, no single source is excluded beforehand. Examples of possible sources are policy documents, archival materials, interviews and participatory observation.

During data collection, the following principles are to be adhered to:

- Multiple sources are prefered to a single source.
- Data should be centralized in a database.
- A chain of evidence needs to be developed in order for external critics to follow the various research phases and steps in the reasoning.

Analysis of the data collected
We focus on two aspects: analysis strategy and quality assurance:

1 *Analysis strategy.* There are three analysis strategies to choose from:
   - A strategy founded on theory-based hypotheses – a hypothesis, derived from a theory, is confirmed or refuted using case data.
   - The rival or competing explanations strategy – two explanations for the observed phenomenon, expressed in terms of the hypotheses of the research design, are confronted with the results from the case.
   - The case description strategy – the case is 'merely' documented and described.
2 *Quality assurance.* During the analysis of the data collected, one must adhere to a strict quality assurance procedure. This quality assurance will be enhanced if one takes into account the following four principles:
   - Pay attention to all data.
   - Pay attention to all possible explanatory factors.
   - In the analysis, focus on the most important aspects of the case.
   - The evaluator must be an expert in the field which he or she is studying.

Reporting of findings
As in all evaluation reports, attention needs to be paid to the target group. Both the content and the formal aspects of the evaluation report need to be geared optimally to the intended audience.

References and Examples

Primary and additional references

Agranoff, R. and Radin, B. (1991) 'The comparative case study approach in public administration', *Research in Public Administration*, vol 1, no 1, pp203–231

Patton, M. Q. (2002) *Qualitative Research and Evaluation Methods*, Sage, Thousand Oaks, CA

Stake, R. E. (1986) 'The case study method in social inquiry', in G. F. Madaus, M. Scriven and D. L. Stufflebeam (eds) *Evaluation Models: Viewpoints on Educational and Human Services Evaluation*, Kluwer-Nijhoff, Boston, MA

Swanborn, P. G. (1999) *Evalueren*, Boom, Amsterdam, The Netherlands

Yin, R. (1994) 'Discovering the future of the case study method in evaluation research', *Evaluation Practice*, vol 15, no 3, pp283–290

Yin, R. (2003a) *Case Study Research: Design and Methods*, Sage, Thousand Oaks, CA

Yin, R. (2003b) *Applications of Case Study Research*, Sage, Thousand Oaks, CA

Examples

Ervin, J. (2003) 'Rapid assessment of protected area management effectiveness in four countries', *BioScience*, vol 53, no 9, pp833–841

This article assesses the management effectiveness of protected areas. It summarizes the results from the implementation of the Rapid Assessment and Prioritization of Protected Area Management (RAPPAM) methodology in four selected countries: Bhutan, China, Russia and South Africa. The most important management issues that affect the management effectiveness of protected areas were identified in order to improve the management strategy.

EEA (2005a) 'Effectiveness of packaging waste management systems in selected countries: An EEA pilot study', http://reports.eea.europa.eu/eea_report_2005_3/en, accessed 1 March 2008

EEA (2005b) 'Effectiveness of urban wastewater treatment policies in selected countries: An EEA pilot study', http://reports.eea.europa.eu/eea_report_2005_2/en, accessed 1 March 2008

Based on earlier work, two pilot case studies on urban wastewater treatment and packaging waste were produced by the European Environmental Agency in 2005. The studies examine how some member states implement certain European Union (EU) policies, investigating the country's institutional and national policy context. The studies' strength lies in detailed examination of the systems that are in place at country level, and the resulting elucidation of features that work well.

3.4 EXPERIMENT AND QUASI-EXPERIMENT

Exemplary evaluation question relating to experiments and quasi-experiments

- Is there a causal relation or at least a correlation between the policy intervention and the anticipated or presumed effect?

3.4.1 Elucidation and context

The essence of the method

What?

Campbell and Stanley (1968) describe experiments as 'the portion of research in which variables are manipulated and their effects upon other variables observed'. An experiment is a means of establishing the causal relationship between element A (in a policy context: policy A) and effect A.

Traditionally, experiments involve two groups, one of which is exposed to the policy intervention that is being studied. The other is the control group. The groups are often composed randomly. A quasi-experiment is an experiment in which one or several conditions for a genuine experiment are not fulfilled.

An experiment has the following characteristics:

- *A causal hypothesis*: the experiment is intended to test a hypothesis regarding a causal relationship between policy and effect.
- *An experimental group and a control group*: the experimental group is exposed to the policy, while the control group is not.
- *Random composition or matching*: the groups are either composed randomly or the members are selected by the evaluator so that both would be identical.
- *Presence of an intervention*: there must always be an intervention or policy implementation.
- *Forcing*: the evaluator determines the composition of the groups. The group members have no say in how the groups are formed.
- *Control over the experiment*: the evaluator controls the process of the experiment and imposes his or her choices regarding the research design upon the participants.

When?

A (quasi-)experiment is conducted to explore the effect of a particular intervention on a certain variable. By means of an experiment, one can provide conclusive evidence of a relationship between an intervention and an effect. Thus, an experiment is appropriate for answering any evaluative question in which causality plays a central role.

In the context of policy evaluation, an experiment is intended to provide insight into the effects of policy, so, obviously, experimentation is an *ex post* approach here.

Advantages and disadvantages?

A (quasi-)experiment offers an important advantage. It is the only method that has the potential to provide certainty regarding causal relationships between a (policy) intervention and an effect.

On the other hand, there are a number of important disadvantages:

- A (quasi-)experiment takes no account of the context. By randomly allocating the members to the groups, one excludes the context as an explanatory variable. Often, however, it is precisely the context that provides part of the explanation.
- In policy evaluation, in general, and environmental policy evaluation, in particular, it does not suffice to ascertain a causal relationship. Certainly, in the case of inadequate effectiveness, one needs to study the actual causes. These causes, which are often situated in the context, are beyond the reach of the experiment. Consequently, an experiment will provide a one-sided view of the policy in question.
- The possibility of randomizing (random allocation of individuals to the experimental and the control groups) depends upon the willingness of those individuals to take part in the experiment. If there is no willingness, then the experiment cannot take place. In the case of policy evaluations, the evaluator is rarely able to make choices about the composition of the groups. The most important reason is that the evaluator cannot intervene in policy-making.
- Some causal relationships are simply too complex to model in an experiment. As explained in Chapter 2, environmental policy is characterized by complexity. Consequently, a (quasi-)experimental evaluation approach on its own is inadequate.
- Side effects are not studied in a (quasi-)experiment. All that one does is manipulate an element and look at the consequences that this generates, either on this element or on a number of elements that have been determined beforehand. Non-anticipated effects are beyond the scope of an experiment.
- The (quasi-)experimental approach is unsuitable for arriving at statements regarding policy processes and the organization of policy implementation. Moreover, (quasi-)experiments take no account of the policy needs. Consequently, the evaluator is unable to make statements regarding the merits and shortcomings of the policy studied.

Historical context

One of the first books on (quasi-)experimental designs in the social sciences was *How To Experiment in Education* by McCall (1923). It was the author's intention to develop a method for gathering experimental data on education policy. A second important contribution to experimental research was published two years later by Fisher (1925) and was entitled *Statistical Methods for Research Workers*. More recently, authors such as Campbell and Stanley (1968), Cook and Campbell (1979) and Cook et al (2002) have written authoritative books on experimental and quasi-experimental research. Each of these authors contributed to the development of the experimental approach. Fisher (1925) complemented the work of McCall (1923) by adding a statistical angle. Campbell, Cook and Stanley, for their part, described the various designs (see below).

Research and evaluation context

Experiments are primarily conducted in laboratory research. Outside a laboratory setting, their field of application is rather limited. In policy research, quasi-experimentation is applied slightly more commonly than experimentation since in the former approach the methodological requirements are less stringent.

In a sense, experimental research stimulated the search for other evaluation methods. After all, the experimental approach often turned out to be inappropriate, impossible or unsuited for evaluation purposes. Such observations inspired many an author to set out in search of alternative methods. Certainly after 1985, the significance of experimentation in evaluation research gradually declined.

3.4.2 Methodology

There are different kinds of experiments. Campbell and Stanley (1968) distinguish between three principal groups:

1 pre-experiments;
2 true experimental designs;
3 quasi-experiments.

The pre-experiments group encompasses one-shot case studies, one group pre-test–post-test design and static group comparison:

- *One-shot case study*: in this approach, one group is studied once prior to the implementation of the policy. The outcome of the case study is used as the baseline measurement.

- *One group pre-test–post-test design*: unlike in the one-shot case study, this approach also includes a measurement after the policy has been implemented.
- *Static-group comparison*: after the policy implementation, one compares a group that has been affected by policy with a group that has not. The composition of the two groups is not necessarily comparable.

The second group is that of the true experimental designs. It encompasses the pre-test–post-test control group design, the Solomon four-group design and the post-test-only control group design:

- *Pre-test–post-test control group design*: this involves measuring the control group and the experimental group before and after the policy intervention. Again, the experimental group is exposed to the policy measure, while the control group is not.
- *Solomon four-group design*: this design involves three control groups, one of which is exposed to the policy programme. The purpose of using three control groups is to eliminate bias caused by awareness of the measurement itself (the so-called measurement effect).
- *Post-test-only control group design*: unlike in a static-group comparison, this design involves two highly comparable groups. As in a static-group comparison, one compares the two groups, one of which has been exposed to policy and one of which has not, after programme implementation.

The third group comprises the quasi-experiments. These are designs where the researcher does not have control over all elements of the experiment. There are various types of quasi-experiments:

- *Time series*: this approach involves a series of measurements before and after the policy intervention.
- *Equivalent sample design*: both experimental group 1 and experimental group 2 are exposed on a regular basis to the policy intervention and are subsequently measured.
- *Equivalent materials samples design*: unlike in the equivalent sample design, a correlating variable is coupled with the policy measure. In other words, the policy measure is paralleled by an event that is assumed to be correlated with the policy measure. Through this coupling, it is possible to eliminate the correlating variable as an explanation for the causal relationship. This creates additional room for studying other possible explanations.
- *Non-equivalent control group design*: an experimental group and a (not necessarily comparable) control group are measured before and after the policy intervention.

- *Counterbalanced designs (also referred to as rotation designs)*: the essence of this approach is that various groups are, in turn, exposed to all policy interventions (if there are several variants).
- *Separate sample pre-test–post-test design*: two comparable groups are measured at two different moments. The control group is measured before the policy intervention, while the experimental group is measured afterwards.

Table 3.1 provides an overview of the various possibilities.

Steps in experiments and quasi-experiments

An experimental design has five characteristics that may also be regarded as five steps in the application of an experiment or quasi-experiment.

Causal hypothesis

First and foremost, a causal hypothesis is formulated. This hypothesis contains expectations with regard to a certain variable before and after the event.

Table 3.1 *Types of experiments and the techniques involved*

Group	Technique
Pre-experiment	One-shot case study
	One group pre-test–post-test
	Static-group comparison
True experiment	Pre-test–post-test control group
	Solomon four group
	Post-test-only control group
Quasi-experiment	Time series
	Equivalent sample
	Equivalent materials samples
	Non-equivalent control group design
	Counterbalanced
	Separate sample pre-test–post-test

Source: inspired by Campbell and Stanley (1968)

Experimental and control group
The second step consists of establishing a control and an experimental group. The experimental group is exposed to the policy intervention, the control group is not. An example of such a design is a situation where municipality A introduces a differentiated rate for waste collection, while municipality B does not.

Random allocation or matching
The groups may be composed randomly or by means of matching. In the latter case, the researcher determines their composition in order to ensure that the two groups have identical characteristics. In the case of randomly composed groups, one strives towards two representative, though not necessarily equivalent, groups. Randomness is supposed to guarantee internal validity.

An intervention
Of course, something either has to happen or not happen. The intervention is the key moment in the experiment. A measurement before or after the intervention of the variable constitutes the basis for establishing whether or not there is a causal relationship between the variable and the intervention.

Control
The researcher needs to control and direct the circumstances, as well as the actual intervention. He or she should pay due attention to the aspect of exclusivity between the experimental and the control group. In other words, it must not be possible for individuals to transfer from one group to the other during the experiment. The researcher must also give due consideration to the allocation of individuals to these groups. The choice between random allocation and matching is a choice which, as we have previously pointed out, should be made by the evaluator.

References and Examples

Primary and additional references

Campbell, D. and Stanley, J. (1968) *Experimental and Quasi-Experimental Designs for Research*, Rand McNally and Company, Chicago, IL

Christensen, L. (1991) *Experimental Methodology*, Allyn and Bacon, Boston, MA

Cook, T. and Campbell, D. (1979) *Quasi-Experimentation*, Houghton Mifflin Company, Boston, MA

Cook, T., Shadish, W. R. and Campbell, D. (2002) *Experimental and Quasi-Experimental Designs for Generalized Causal Inference*, 2nd edition, Houghton Mifflin Company, Boston, MA

Fisher, R.A. (1925) *Statistical Methods for Research Workers*, Oliver and Boyd, Edinburgh, UK

Frondel, M. and Schmidt, C. M. (2005) 'Evaluating environmental programs: The perspective of modern evaluation research', *Ecological Economics*, vol 55, no 4, pp515–526

Madaus, G., Scriven, M. and Stufflebeam, D. (1983) *Evaluation Models*, Kluwer-Nijhoff, Boston, MA

McCall, W.A. (1923) *How To Experiment in Education*, Macmillan, New York

Examples

Cason, T. N. (1995) 'An experimental investigation of the seller incentives in the EPA's emission trading auction', *The American Economic Review*, vol 85, no 4, pp905–922

This article discusses an experimental system for emission trading in which buyers receive the same incentives as sellers. The experiment made it possible to examine how actors behaved in a situation that contrasts with the dominant policy in which sellers with the lowest asking prices receive the highest bids.

Carlsson, F. and Kataria, M. (2006) 'Assessing management options for weed control with demanders and non-demanders in a choice experiment', *Working Papers in Economics*, Department of Economics, Göteborg, www.handels.gu.se/epc/archive/00004892/01/ gunwpe0208.pdf, accessed 1 March 2008

The *Nymphoides peltata* is an aquatic plant classified as a serious weed in Sweden. Like other aquatic weeds, it was initially introduced for its appealing appearance and colourful flower. Because of gradually overgrown water bodies, which interfere with boat traffic and recreational activities, the plant has become a nuisance. The purpose of this paper is to estimate the benefits of a weed management programme and to compare them with the corresponding costs. A choice experiment study is made to investigate the benefits of various management strategies. The authors opt for a choice experiment and not a contingent valuation survey because they are interested in measuring the willingness to pay for a number of attributes of the management options.

3.5 FORMATIVE/DEVELOPMENTAL EVALUATION

Exemplary evaluation questions relating to formative/developmental evaluation

- Are the policies effective?
- Why does policy succeed or fail in attaining its goals?

3.5.1 Elucidation and context

The essence of the method

What?

In formative evaluation, one studies the 'operationalization' and implementation of policy, and makes an assessment of the quality of policy-making, the organizational context, the policy implementers, policy organization and policy processes. A formative evaluation aims to formulate recommendations on the basis of which policy can be adjusted. For this reason, the method is also commonly referred to as developmental evaluation.

The methodology reveals divergences between policy on paper and policy in practice, identifies strengths and weaknesses of policy, points out bottlenecks and opportunities, and makes suggestions for a better policy implementation. Formative evaluation takes due account of the dynamic policy context and tries to restrict the changeability of policy – which is inherent in complex and varied projects in a fluid policy environment:

> *Formative evaluations focus not on the products of a program* per se, *but on the internal dynamics of all that contributes to (or hinders) the production of that product or outcome.* (Rist, 1990, p36)

As a result, formative evaluation is concerned primarily with policy implementation, but not only that. The evaluator can also apply the method to gain insight into the programme theory, the policy outcome and policy impact.

Formative evaluation is most commonly applied to satisfy the information needs of policy-makers. Increasingly, however, it assumes a more participatory quality. Stakeholders are involved in the evaluation of policy. In this sense, the role of the evaluator is extended: he or she not only generates and communicates evaluation findings, but also involves a variety of actors in the study. They are invited, as it were, to reflect on their own practical knowledge about, and experiences with the issue, to discuss these issues and to reach an evaluative conclusion together.

When?

Formative evaluations can be an important management instrument if the object of evaluation is complex and relatively impenetrable, if the political sensitivity surrounding the topic is great, or if the policy issue itself is subject to constant change. In this respect, it is important that the evaluator should monitor carefully in which way policy and policy circumstances are changing.

Formative evaluation may be applied in various phases of the policy cycle. It can be useful in the phase of policy preparation (e.g. in order to analyse policy needs), but also in the phase of policy implementation (in order to make adjustments). Proponents of the approach often advise that formative evaluation should be structurally incorporated within the organization of policy.

Advantages and disadvantages?

Formative evaluation offers the following advantages:

- Formative evaluation can paint a detailed picture of a policy, while that policy is subject to constant change.
- Formative evaluation allows one to draw conclusions with regard to the functioning of existing policy, as well as future policy projects. In other words, formative evaluation is a method that can be applied *ex post* as well as *ex ante*.
- Formative evaluation supplements classical evaluation methods that emphasize goal attainment. Formative evaluation is essential to understanding why policy is successful or not, and which complex factors contribute in this regard.
- Formative or developmental evaluation can result in a modification and further optimization of policy. An important condition is, however, that policy-makers and other relevant parties should be prepared to take findings on board. It is not inconceivable that policy-makers may revoke support for the evaluation if it emerges that the causes of policy failure or inertia lie in weaknesses in policy implementation or design.
- If one takes a participatory approach to formative evaluation, then it can help to enhance group cohesion among the policy actors and result in joint learning. Participatory formative evaluation can work as a catalyst as the group is encouraged to think together about ways of optimizing policy. An added bonus is that this contributes to capacity-building.

There are also a number of disadvantages to take into account:

- Formative evaluation is time consuming and labour intensive. It is primarily based on a qualitative approach that is a heavy burden on the evaluator in terms of both time and intensity.
- This qualitative approach also makes formative evaluation rather vulnerable. The use of qualitative research methods can disappoint the target group of

the evaluation, especially if they are expecting solid conclusions on the basis of quantitative data.

Historical context

As an evaluation method, formative evaluation is known as the polar opposite of summative evaluation. Formative and summative evaluation are considered archetypes of policy evaluation in the Anglo-Saxon (primarily American) evaluation literature. While they have no unequivocal significance in the field of evaluation, consensus has it that formative evaluation is aimed at the development and optimization of policy programmes, while summative evaluation is primarily concerned with the collection of information on the efficacy of policy. Formative evaluation is more action oriented, while summative evaluation tends to be more research oriented.

Research and evaluation context

Chelimsky (in Patton, 1997, p65) makes a distinction between three objectives of evaluation research, which are at once indicative of the perspective from which those evaluations are developed:

1   evaluations that are intended to substantiate policy and are based on the perspective of accountability;
2   evaluations that are aimed at policy improvement and that are drawn up from a developmental perspective; and
3   evaluations for academic purposes that start from the perspective of generating knowledge.

Formative evaluation belongs to the second type (i.e. the group of improvement-oriented evaluation studies).

3.5.2 Methodology

Steps in formative evaluation

Ideally, formative evaluation should involve six steps:

1   debate on the value of formative evaluation;
2   *ex ante* inclusion of formative evaluation;
3   stimulating success factors;
4   pre-study of policy;
5   data collection and processing; and
6   valorization of research findings.

Debate on the value of formative evaluation

Authorities and policy stakeholders (at all levels) should agree that formative evaluation is an appropriate strategy towards collective learning and policy adjustment. This will, among other things, require negotiation over access to, and use of, information on policy, agreement on a distribution of tasks, and clarity with regard to the goals of the evaluation.

Ex ante inclusion of formative evaluation

The evaluation should be provided for in the policy design so that it is accepted as an essential means of monitoring policy and making adjustments in accordance with changing circumstances. This implies, among other things, that a foundation for formative evaluation can be laid in an early stage of the needs analysis (see Section 3.1 'Needs analysis') and evaluability assessment (see Section 4.7 'Evaluability assessment').

Stimulating success factors

Circumstances must be created in which formative evaluation flourishes. This implies, among other things, that one should cooperate with the clients of the evaluation on the development of a culture that stimulates policy learning; the provision of open communication channels that are conducive to a smooth information flow; the creation of opportunities for constructing a common knowledge base; and the adaptation of systems and structures that hinder policy learning.

Pre-study of policy

Information is collected on the history of and the state of affairs in developing the policy; the various parties involved in the policy; and their information needs and interests. This requires interviews of policy-makers at the central level, local policy-makers and policy implementers, as well as members of the target group. Each respondent is presented with questions about his or her evaluation needs and expectations with regard to the ongoing evaluation study.

Data collection and processing

Formative evaluation requires constant collection and processing of policy data. The choice of method for data collection depends upon the evaluation questions that are being asked and the preference of those involved in the evaluation process. Usually, one applies data triangulation (i.e. data are obtained from different sources).

Valorization of research findings

Should an evaluator merely make the findings known and stimulate learning processes or should he or she also play a role in the valorization of the evaluation?

Opinions differ. If it is an external evaluator, his or her assignment usually ends after the finalization of the evaluation report. If he or she is an internal evaluator, then there is a greater likelihood that he or she will also be involved in managing the learning processes within the organization. Formative evaluation should always result in an in-depth study of the policy programme. Therefore, the method is best combined with the case study approach.

References and Examples

Primary and additional references

EVALSED (undated) 'Formative evaluation', www.evalsed.info/downloads/sb2_formative_evaluation.doc, accessed 1 March 2008

Patton, M. Q. (1994) 'Developmental evaluation', *Evaluation Practice*, vol 15, no 3, pp311–319

Patton, M. Q. (1997) *Utilization-Focused Evaluation: The New Century Text*, Sage, Thousand Oaks, CA

Preskill, H. and Torres, R. T. (2000) 'The learning dimension of evaluation use', *New Directions for Evaluation*, no 88, pp25–37

Rist, R. C. (ed) (1990) *Policy and Program Evaluation: Perspectives on Design and Utilization*, (publisher unknown), Brussels, Belgium

Examples

Esters, O., Montgomery, D. and Oakland, M. (2007) 'A formative evaluation of the pick a better snack campaign: Results of parent focus groups', *Journal of the American Dietetic Association*, vol 107, no 8, pA93

This article assesses a campaign promoting fruits and vegetables. The purpose of this evaluation was to determine the attitudes, perceptions and opinions of parents with school-aged children towards this campaign. Seventy parents with different backgrounds participated in the evaluation research. They were invited, for example, to express their opinion on how the campaign could be improved.

Chacon-Moscoso, S., Anguera-Argilaga, M. T., Antonio, J., Gil, P. and Holgado-Tello, F. P. (2002) 'A mutual catalytic role of formative evaluation: The interdependent roles of evaluators and local programme practitioners', *Evaluation*, vol 8, no 4, pp413–432

This article describes the 'mutual catalytic model' of programme design and formative evaluation. In this model of formative evaluation, local practitioners help to specify programme goals and improve evaluation, while evaluators help to elaborate programme goals and evaluation needs. The model is exemplified using experiences with homeless childcare centres in Seville, Spain.

3.6 GOAL-FREE EVALUATION (GFE)

Exemplary evaluation question relating to goal-free evaluation

• Is this policy 'right'?

Note that the qualification 'right' may involve different criteria, especially those that are not reflected in policy documents (see Chapter 2).

3.6.1 Elucidation and context

The essence of the method

What?

Goal-free evaluation (GFE) diverges from other evaluation approaches, which are mainly goal-based, in that, if applied strictly, the evaluator is initially unaware of the purpose the object of study is supposed to serve. In a less strict interpretation of the method, the evaluator takes no account of those objectives, but may be aware of them. Consequently, the evaluator will need to look at what the object of study (the policy programme) actually does, rather than concentrate on what it is assumed or expected to do.

In goal-free evaluation, the scope of vision of the evaluator (and, thus, the object of the evaluation study) is purposely kept as broad as possible. This has no repercussions in terms of the amount of attention that is paid to the (formal policy) objectives. After all, if policy produces the expected effects, then this will transpire from the evaluation. However, if the policy programme fails to achieve as expected, or if it has other (unforeseen) effects, then this, too, will emerge from the study.

If the evaluator is able to evaluate the policy programme entirely independently, there will be no prior agreements regarding the evaluation criteria to be applied. However, the evaluator is rarely truly independent. If the study has been commissioned, the best possible approach is to combine different evaluation criteria (i.e. those that the party requesting the evaluation finds important and those that the policy stakeholders, or impacted population, judge to be significant).

When?

Goal-free evaluation assesses the effects of the policy programme on the basis of evaluation criteria. This implies that the method can only be applied *ex post*, after implementation of the policy programme.

Advantages and disadvantages?
One of the main arguments in favour of this method is that, certainly in its purest form, it allows the evaluator to detect side effects. The rationale behind the approach is that an evaluator who need not pay attention to the policy objectives will tend to look more thoroughly for possible effects and, as the case may be, side effects.

A second important advantage is that the evaluator is able to select the evaluation criteria independently (at least, in the strict variant of the method), and is not restricted by whoever has commissioned the study or by criteria determined by the policy objectives.

Scriven (1990, p180) sums up the other advantages:

*   GFE avoids expensive and time-consuming efforts to identify and evaluate policy objectives (unlike in the case of programme theory evaluation; see Section 3.2). Consequently, more attention can be paid to the effects of policy.
*   GFE has a more limited impact upon policy activities. Since the evaluator is detached from the policy-makers and more closely aligned with the target group and other stakeholders, there is less interaction between evaluator and policy-makers. Consequently, these policy-makers are far less involved in the evaluation study than is the case with other methods.
*   GFE takes due account of changing needs and goals. Since GFE does not take formal objectives as a starting point, it can incorporate actual policy expectations and needs within the evaluation.
*   GFE is less prone to bias or influencing by the policy-makers as there is less interaction between evaluator and policy-makers.
*   One can, at all times, make the switch to a goal-based evaluation. In contrast, it is not possible to switch from a goal-based evaluation to a goal-free approach. In a goal-based evaluation, the evaluator works in the light of the policy objectives. In other words, those objectives are known to the evaluator, so that he or she is subsequently unable to be detached from this knowledge.
*   There is a reduced likelihood that the evaluation will be influenced by the (unconscious) tendency to try to please the client who has commissioned the study. Since the evaluator is unaware of the policy objectives, he or she runs a smaller risk of turning in a positively biased evaluation.

A disadvantage of goal-free evaluation is that it can be very hard to create a situation where the evaluator is entirely unaware of the policy objectives. Therefore, a less strict interpretation of GFE is often the highest achievable. In this approach, the evaluation criteria are still chosen by the evaluator, but he or she is also aware of the policy objectives.

Another drawback of goal-free evaluation is that the method can create confusion with regard to the criteria on which policy ought to be evaluated. In classical (goal-based) evaluations, attaining the formal policy objectives is considered to be the central evaluation criterion. In the case of goal-free evaluation, other criteria are involved: criteria put forward by the evaluator and criteria suggested by the policy stakeholders. These criteria can be multifarious and, moreover, contradictory.

Historical context

Goal-free evaluation was introduced by Scriven in 1972. He proposed the method for two reasons. First, he considered it to be more important to pay attention to all real, tangible effects than to presumed effects (i.e. the envisaged policy outcomes). Second, he saw GFE as a way of avoiding the classical evaluator problem of a lack of clear and unequivocal objectives.

Research and evaluation context

Goal-free evaluation is an important method of evaluation research because it gave rise to one of the most prominent debates within the evaluation community. The debate on the position of formal objectives in a policy programme evaluation only really emerged after the introduction of this approach.

Despite the significance of goal-free evaluation in academic discussions on policy evaluation, GFE is not particularly popular among evaluators and commissioners of such studies. It is not popular among evaluators because of its lack of a clear structure, while it is unpopular among those commissioning evaluation studies because it pays no specific attention to the policy objectives and because it poses the potential threat of uncovering implicit goals and side effects of policy. As a compromise, one might opt for a hybrid form, such as goal-free front-end evaluation. Here, one persists with a GFE up to the interim evaluation report. Then, after feedback has been provided, one proceeds with a goal-based approach and incorporates the policy objectives within the evaluation and, consequently, within the eventual evaluation report.

Since GFE applies policy needs rather than policy objectives as criteria, it ties in closely with the philosophy of needs analysis (see Section 3.1 'Needs analysis').

3.6.2 Methodology

Steps in goal-free evaluation

Four steps are distinguished in goal-free evaluation, as outlined in Box 3.5.

Evaluation design

First, an evaluation design is worked out. In other words, a selection is made of methods and techniques for evaluating the intended object. The evaluation design needs to take into account the manner in which data are to be collected and analysed. Furthermore, all (sub)steps in data collection and analysis should be incorporated within the operational planning of the evaluation study. This planning should ideally encompass information on both financial aspects and time spending.

BOX 3.5 THE FOUR STEPS IN GOAL-FREE EVALUATION

1   Design of the evaluation.
2   Selection of the evaluator.
3   Goal-free evaluation/study.
4   Formulation of policy recommendations.

Source: adapted from Scriven (1991)

Selection of the evaluator

When selecting an evaluator, it is important to bear in mind that he or she should be able to embark on the evaluation of the policy programme without prior knowledge of the formal policy objectives. The evaluator is, almost by definition, not an expert in the policy topics in which the evaluation unfolds. In this way, a maximum distance is kept between the evaluator and the goals to be achieved.

The evaluator is part of a team of evaluators, each of whom has areas of thematic expertise. This is required because the initial evaluator is supposed to evaluate policy without prior knowledge of the policy to be considered. In order to be able to interpret findings adequately, it is therefore necessary to subsequently bring in team members who are knowledgeable in the policy field in question.

The evaluator should preferably be experienced. This is recommended because he or she must be able to rely on their own methodological expertise during the exploration of (side) effects.

Goal-free evaluation/study

This step encompasses the actual study or evaluation. The data collection and analysis techniques selected in step 1 (design of the evaluation; see Box 3.5) are now applied. Depending upon the policy effects identified by the evaluator, criteria are formulated to assess these outcomes. According to Scriven (1991), the stakeholder needs should take precedence in this respect.

Formulation of policy recommendations

The final step consists in formulating policy recommendations. This happens on the basis of the evaluation outcomes. Since this evaluation method takes account of all effects and consequences of policy, the policy recommendations may be expected to be broader and deeper than in the case of goal-based evaluation.

References and Examples

Primary and additional references

Alkin, M. (1972) 'Wider context goals and goals-based evaluators: Evaluation comment', *The Journal of Educational Evaluation*, vol 3, no 4, pp10–11

Kneller, G. (1972) 'Goal-free evaluation: Evaluation comment', *The Journal of Educational Evaluation*, vol 3, no 4, pp13–15

Patton, M. Q. (1997) *Utilization-Focused Evaluation*, Sage, Thousand Oaks, CA

Popham, J. (1972) 'Results rather than rethoric. Evaluation comment', *The Journal of Educational Evaluation*, vol 3, no 4, pp12–13

Scriven, M. (1972) 'Pros and cons about goal-free evaluation. Evaluation comment', *The Journal of Educational Evaluation*, vol 3, no 4, pp1–7

Scriven, M. (1991) *Evaluation Thesaurus*, Sage, Newbury Park, CA

Stufflebeam, D. L. (1972) 'Should or could evalution be goal-free? Evaluation comment', *The Journal of Educational Evaluation*, vol 3, no 4, pp7–9

Examples

Kilvington, M. (1998) 'The Whaingaroa catchment management project', www.land careresearch.co.nz/research/sustainablesoc/social/whaingaroa2.asp, accessed 1 March 2008

This webpage refers to a goal-free evaluation of an integrated environmental management system in New Zealand in order to assess the real effects of this system in a pilot project.

Lay, M. and Papadopoulos, I. (2007) 'An exploration of fourth generation evaluation in practice', *Evaluation*, vol 13, no 4, pp495–504

This article explores the applicability of some of the main principles of fourth-generation evaluation (see Section 4.4 'Constructivist evaluation') in relation to an evaluation undertaken by the authors. In line with a constructivist evaluation methodology, the evaluation did not have predetermined goals against which to measure outcomes, outputs or processes; rather, the authors set out to describe the project using what is termed a 'thick description'. In this way, the evaluation strongly resembles goal-free evaluation.

3.7 IMPACT ASSESSMENTS

Impact assessments are intended to provide information about the effects of policy even before its implementation. The type of policy concerned may vary. Traditionally, construction projects for a new motorway, a mining site, a large industrial site or a dam are regarded to be the type of programme where an impact assessment is appropriate. However, policy measures or policy programmes can also be subjected to an impact assessment.

The best-known type of impact assessment is a social impact assessment (SIA). However, this is not the oldest form of impact assessment. It was, in fact, the 1969 National Environmental Policy Act (NEPA) in the US which created a legal basis for environmental impact statements (EISs). SIAs emerged slightly later, in 1973, as one came to realize that the social aspect of certain projects had been somewhat overlooked. The third offspring is regulatory impact assessment (RIA). Like environmental impact assessments (EIAs), the RIA was provided with a legal basis in the US with the introduction of 1981 Executive Order E.O. 12291. In what follows, we provide the reader with more detailed information on these three types of impact assessment, leaving behind other types of assessments such as health, spatial and integrated impact assessments that became increasingly popular during the last decade or so.

3.7.1 Social Impact Assessment

Exemplary evaluation questions relating to social impact assessment

- Does policy have a positive or a negative impact upon particular societal processes, and with what consequences?
- What are the expected (side) effects of policy in specific areas? How should we assess those effects? Are they positive or negative?

3.7.1.1 Elucidation and context

The essence of the method

What?

Social impact assessment is a method for identifying which social changes will occur if a certain project or policy is implemented. The motivation for carrying out an SIA is the need to be able to anticipate social consequences that may have been neglected during the planning phase of a policy or project. The essence of an SIA lies in comparing the object studied with similar objects on which more information is available.

When?

An SIA is carried out *ex ante* after the planning phase, but before the implementation phase. Thanks to this timing, an SIA may serve different purposes: on the one hand, an SIA will try to predict the effects of a project or policy, while, on the other, it can be used to identify possible undesired side effects. A third purpose is to allow one to anticipate such effects. This objective is not mentioned explicitly in the literature; but it is quite apparent from the methods and applications of SIA.

Advantages and disadvantages?

The main advantage of the method is that it approaches the research question very thoroughly and in a structured fashion. The step-by-step approach that is detailed below illustrates this. There is, however, a downside to the approach – namely, that it is extremely time consuming. Moreover, like most other methods, it provides no guarantee that the social effects have been evaluated exhaustively.

Historical context

SIAs were first applied in 1973 in the US. Since 1969, there was an obligation under the so-called NEPA legislation to draw up an environmental impact statement (EIS) in certain cases. Neglect of the social implications of projects for which an EIS was mandatory would eventually result in the introduction of the SIA approach.

Research and evaluation context

The SIA belongs to the group of *ex ante* evaluations. It has come to occupy an important place in the world of policy evaluation. The method has an Anglo-Saxon background, as is apparent not only from the examples listed within the references at the end of the chapter but also from the organizations concerned with SIAs. These organizations are found almost exclusively in the Anglophone world. One of the best-known is the International Association for Impact Assessment (see www.iaia.org).

The scope for applying SIAs has expanded over the years. Where the emphasis used to be very much on the use of SIAs in projects, it is now acceptable to incorporate SIAs within policy programmes, in general, on the condition, however, that the object of study (i.e. the policy or project) has been adequately delineated.

3.7.1.2 Methodology

The basis of SIAs lies in the comparison of the project or policy under study with a comparable past experience. The validity of the findings depends upon the degree of similarity and comparability. In order to satisfy these criteria, data are collected at four levels:

1   project parameters: information about the project;
2   information on the institutions that keep periodic statistics (census and secondary demographic data);
3   municipal information on local characteristics (i.e. community/county data);
4   information from the stakeholders (i.e. public involvement data).

These data are subsequently entered in a model. Two versions are used. First, there is the basic model, which compares between the past and the future project. Second, an extended model is used that is comprised of the basic model plus the control group.

On the basis of five criteria, the comparability of the past and the future project is tested (see Box 3.6). The changes that are studied are expressed as 26 variables. These variables may undergo an impact during four phases of the project or policy programme: the planning and development phase; the construction and implementation phase; the implementation and maintenance phase; and the termination and phase-out phase. The list of 26 variables can be found in Burdge (1994, p43).

BOX 3.6 THE FIVE BASIC CRITERIA
IN SOCIAL IMPACT ASSESSMENT

1   Population impacts.
2   Community/institutional arrangements.
3   Conflicts between local residents and newcomers.
4   Individual and family-level impacts.
5   Community infrastructure needs.

Source: adapted from Burdge (1994, p43)

Steps in SIA

The methodology consists of ten steps:

1   public participation;
2   inventory of alternatives;
3   baseline measurement;
4   scoping;
5   prediction of effects;

6 prediction of possible responses to expected effects;
7 indirect and cumulative effects;
8 changes relating to alternatives;
9 compensation;
10 monitoring.

Public participation

The purpose of this step is to involve all stakeholders in the evaluation procedure. To this end, a public involvement plan is used. Possible stakeholders are actors who may hear, smell or see the effects; actors living in the vicinity or having an interest even though they live further away; and actors who are forced to relocate. The following groups may be added to the list: actors suffering loss of land use because of the project or programme, as well as actors who may experience a range of indirect or derived effects. Once the actors have been identified, representatives of these groups are invited to participate in the planning and decision procedure. The active involvement of representatives is preferable to a public hearing.

Inventory of alternatives

The proposed policy options and possible alternatives are described in detail. The variables considered provide information about the location, land use, public services, scope of the project and employment, need for local workers and public administration resources.

Baseline measurement

In this step, the evaluator describes the social context prior to the policy or project. This context shall be described more extensively in the case of a policy programme than in the case of a project. Some of the necessary focal points are the relationship between the social context and the biophysical environment; the historical and social context; and the cultural and socio-psychological characteristics of the affected population.

Scoping

The evaluator makes a selection of possible social effects to be studied. This should happen in collaboration with the actors selected in step 1 (public participation). The following approaches may be applied to this end: literature study, written survey and a range of participatory techniques.

Prediction of effects

In this step, a comparison is made between expected results in the case of changed and unchanged policy. A number of methods can be applied here:

- comparative methods;
- trend extrapolation based on projections (using empirical data regarding existing policy, predictions are made in relation to the policy under study);
- multiplier methods based on population data;
- scenarios (different options are translated into policy scenarios, which are substantiated predictions);
- expert testimonies (on the basis of the opinion of one or more experts, a prediction is made of the expected effects);
- computer models (expected or measured values are entered into a computer model; the output is an elucidation of the expected evolution of these and other variables);
- calculation of 'lost future' (irreversible effects) – an estimation of the opportunity cost (i.e. the cost of foregoing an opportunity as well as the benefits that could be received from that opportunity).

Prediction of possible responses to expected effects

In this step, one considers the possible responses of those directly affected by the project or policy programme. A distinction is made between attitudes and behaviours. Comparative methods are particularly useful in this step of the evaluation. Basing one's assessment on attitudes only would result in a distorted image, as both negative and positive appraisals tend to be expressed more easily through attitudes than through behaviours.

Indirect and cumulative effects

In this phase, attention is paid to the effects that do not manifest themselves directly and/or nearby. Although they are hard to assess, such effects can be very important. After all, frequently, these 'hidden' effects have not been anticipated. By paying special attention to identifying them, one can gain better insight into their significance.

Changes relating to alternatives

Any adjustments to the project or policy programme should be submitted to the above study procedure from step 5 (prediction of effects).

Compensation

Attenuation of the negative effects is an integral part of SIA. This implies anticipating the side effects through *ex ante* compensatory measures.

Monitoring

The final step consists of establishing a monitoring system. The purpose of this system is to detect any unexpected effects. On this basis, one is able to adjust the

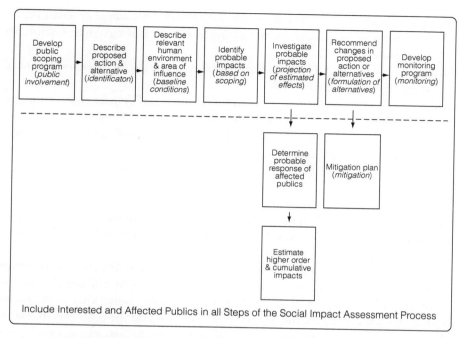

Figure 3.1   *Step-by-step approach to social impact assessment*

Source: Burdge (2004, p104); reproduced with permission of the author and the publisher

programme/project, as well as monitor yields data that may be used in future SIAs for similar projects or programmes.

In visual terms, the step-by-step approach is depicted in Figure 3.1.

Remarks

Techniques and methods that may be used in combination with this approach are pilot studies, the Delphi technique, multi-criteria analysis (see Section 3.10), cost-benefit analysis and cost-effectiveness analysis (see Section 3.8), fiscal impact analysis, input–output analysis and the logframe method (see Section 3.9).

References and Examples

Primary and additional references

Barrow, C. J. (1997) *Environmental and Societal Impact Assessment: An Introduction*, Wiley and Sons, New York, NY

Becker, H. A. (1997) *Social Impact Assessment: Method and Experience in Europe, North America and the Developing World*, UCL Press, London

Becker, H. A. and Vanclay, F. (2003) *The International Handbook of Social Impact Assessment: Conceptual and Methodological Advances*, Edward Elgar Publishing, Cheltenham, UK

Burdge, R. J. (1994) *A Conceptual Approach to Social Impact Assessment*, Social Ecology Press, Middleton, WI

Burdge, R. J. (2004) *A Conceptual Approach to Social Impact Assessment*, 3rd edition, Social Ecology Press, Middleton, WI

Vanclay, F. and Bronstein, D. A. (1995) *Environmental and Social Impact Assessment*, Wiley and Sons, Chichester, UK

Examples

Juslén, J. (1997), 'Social impact assessment in transportation system planning', http://info.stakes.fi/NR/rdonlyres/B33E019F-F04A-47BF-A4E5-7E12BC491104/0/siatransport. pdf, accessed 1 March 2008

In 1996, a prestudy was carried out to investigate how the social perspective has been taken into account in transportation planning in Finland during the recent past. The objectives of the study were to achieve a broad view of the social impacts that are examined, the methods that are used and the problems that arise when assessing transportation systems. This study was the first step in developing an SIA process that could be integrated within transportation system planning.

Marx, A. (2002), 'Uncertainty and social impacts: A case study of a Belgian village', *Environmental Impact Assessment Review*, vol 22, no 1, pp79–96

This article describes a social impact assessment that was conducted in a small village on the left side of the River Scheldt near Antwerp, Belgium. The aim was to estimate the impact of the construction of a container dock (for the expansion of the port of Antwerp) on the sociological profile of the village. It was concluded that the social impact upon the socio-demographic profile of the village, the number of associations, and the number of businesses will be very significant. Many people are leaving or intend to leave the village, associations will lose members and businesses will lose customers.

3.7.2 Environmental Impact Assessment (EIA)

Exemplary evaluation question relating to environmental impact assessment

- Which environmental changes will occur as a result of the implementation/execution of a particular project or policy programme or strategy?

3.7.2.1 Elucidation and context

The essence of the method

What?

Environmental impact assessment (EIA) is a method where one evaluates the expected effects of a policy programme in order to allow preventative adjustments. Leroy (1996, p11) asserts that environmental impact assessments not only predict future effects, but also outline possible alternatives. Consequently, EIAs are also a tool that policy-makers can use to weigh up policy alternatives.

Like SIAs, EIAs were originally developed for application in large-scale infrastructure works. Today, the EIA is applied much more broadly to assess the potential environmental harm of policy programmes and projects. In many countries, the EIA is a legal-administrative procedure where, before an activity or intervention (projects, policy plans and programmes) takes place, the environmental consequences are studied, discussed and evaluated.

When?

An EIA is conducted *ex ante*. Since it aims to predict effects and anticipate these predictions, the method is applied before policy is put into practice.

Advantages and disadvantages?

The main advantage of the method is that it approaches the research question very thoroughly and in a structured fashion. The step-by-step approach that is outlined below illustrates this. There is, however, a downside to the approach – namely, that it is extremely time consuming. Moreover, like most other methods, it provides no guarantee that the environmental effects have been evaluated exhaustively.

Historical context

The US has had NEPA legislation, which imposes the obligation to write an environmental impact statement (EIS), since 1969. In Europe, countries such as

Germany, Ireland and France followed the American example in the course of the 1970s. In 1985, the European Commission introduced Directive 85/337/EC, which was subsequently amended in 1997 (Directive 1997/11/EU) and 2001 (Directive 2001/42/EU).

Research and evaluation context

EIA belongs to the group of *ex ante* evaluations. It has come to occupy an important place in the world of policy evaluation. More so than SIA, EIA is institutionally embedded in the European Union and its member states. Within the developing world, Asia emerged at the forefront of establishing EIA practices. For example, China has a history of more than 20 years of experience with EIAs. In sharp contrast, environmental legislation is currently often lacking in Africa. It is remarkable that the scope of application of EIAs has expanded over the years. It is now accepted as suitable for evaluating policy programmes on the condition that the object of evaluation has been adequately delineated.

3.7.2.2 Methodology

We consider the various steps involved in EIAs according to the American model that is laid down by the US Environmental Protection Agency (EPA). In what follows, we reconstruct the various steps using Barrow (1997).

The EPA distinguishes between phases 0 and 6, as outlined in Box 3.7.

BOX 3.7 PHASES 0 TO 6 OF AN EIA ACCORDING TO THE US ENVIRONMENTAL PROTECTION AGENCY

The phases are as follows:

0 = Screening.
1 = Scoping.
2 = Impact assessment.
3 = Scrutiny.
4 = Decision.
5 = Implementation.
6 = Monitoring.

Phases 0 and 3 to 6 are policy phases. Phases 1 and 2 are evaluation phases. For the purpose of this handbook, we will consider those evaluation phases of the EPA's model of EIA in some greater detail.

Scoping

Scoping is the phase in which the EIA is delineated. This requires that one determines precisely which effects are to be studied; what purpose the EIA is intended to serve; what are its boundaries, its timeframe and its strategy; who will conduct the EIA; and what level of detail shall be involved. In other words, the scoping phase determines the focus of the EIA.

It is generally assumed that a brainstorming session with experts is the most time-efficient way of going about scoping. These experts are assumed to provide the necessary input for delimiting the object of study. Kennedy and Ross (1992) argue for continuous scoping. By this they mean to indicate that an (E)IA will benefit from flexible boundaries and that a shifting focus should therefore be possible. They see scoping in the context of identifying the impact, the assessment of the impact and controlling any (unwanted) impacts (see below). This form of applied scoping leads to focused environmental assessment.

Scoping is important for sustaining the focus of the (E)IA. If scoping does not lead to a clearly delineated EIA, then one runs the danger that the assessment might assume encyclopaedic proportions. Such an extensive scope is not only untenable in practice, but it also rarely fits into the policy timeframe.

As scoping is concerned with the selection of a number of specific questions, the risk of subjectivity and arbitrariness is rather great. Therefore, Barrow (1997) suggests that key actors from within and outside policy circles be involved in the process.

Impact assessment

We may subdivide this phase into four steps:

1 *Identification of the impact.* In this phase, one determines whether a possible impact has been overlooked. For a number of commonly studied objects, checklists have been drawn up. New objects for EIA require additional approaches, such as surveys, observations, literature studies, expert interviews, workshops and public consultations.

   Impact is subdivided into direct impact, indirect impact and cumulated impact:
   - Direct impacts occur in the immediate vicinity and as a result of policy.
   - Indirect and cumulative impacts occur further along the causal chain of events and may be likened to second- and third-order effects (i.e. knock-on effects of the first-order effects).
   - Cumulated impacts are subdivided into aggregated impact and synergetic impacts. Both are the combined result of other impacts. In the case of synergetic impact, the overall impact does not equal the sum of the individual impacts. There is, in other words, an additional factor to take into account.

Crucial in this phase is the availability of baseline data. This is the description of the situation before the project or policy programme was put into practice.

2   *Assessment of the value.* There are no universal rules for determining the value of impacts. The evaluator can proceed on the basis of a number of characteristics. Statistical significance, ecological value and social value can all help to determine the overall value/significance of an impact. However, impact evaluation invariably involves an aspect of subjectivity. For this reason, it is important that one should strive for the greatest possible degree of transparency. In this context, we should warn of the dangers of quantification. By expressing the value of the impact in terms of an index, ranking or a monetary equivalent, they assume a semblance of objectivity. The reasoning behind the quantification, which tends to be subjective, is often unclear or unknown. Nevertheless, quantification of impacts is an important step in their assessment. Barrow (1997, Chapter 5) mentions the 'environmental evaluations system' as a method for quantification. Cost-benefit analysis is also a good example of a monetary quantification method.

3   *Assessment of the likelihood.* In this phase, one puts the predicted effect in its proper societal context. This step is necessary in order to asses the likelihood that the effect will manifest itself in that context. Barrow (1997) does not explain in greater detail how one should proceed. Modelling is an obvious approach. Although far from a flawless technique, using a simulation model can certainly be worthwhile. For one thing, it enables the evaluator to make predictions regarding future connected events. As models are appropriate for dealing with dynamic processes, they also provide ample room for taking into account factors of uncertainty that are inherent in EIAs.

4   *Predictions regarding the manifestation of the impact.* This step is a synthesis of the preceding steps. Its purpose is to arrive at an assessment of the impacts on the basis of value and likelihood.

References and Examples

Primary and additional references

Barrow, C. J. (1997) *Environmental and Societal Impact Assessment: An Introduction*, Wiley and Sons, New York, NY

Bonte, R., Leroy, P. and Mooren, R. (eds) (1996) *Milieueffectrapportage*, Aeneas, Amsterdam, The Netherlands

Kennedy, A. J. and Ross, W. A. (1992) 'An approach to integrate impact scoping with environmental impact assessment', *Environmental Management*, vol 16, no 4, pp475–484

Examples

Geneletti, D. (2008) 'Impact assessment of proposed ski areas: A GIS approach integrating biological, physical and landscape indicators', *Environmental Impact Assessment Review*, vol 28, pp116–130

Ski centres are characterized by significant environmental impacts that occur during both the construction and the operation phase. In Trentino, a ski destination located in northern Italy, new ski areas were identified by planning tools. This article presents a study to assess and compare the impacts of the proposed ski areas within two valleys strongly linked to winter tourism: the Fiemme and Fassa valleys. The method is based on the computation of spatial indicators to predict and quantify critical impacts, such as ecosystem loss and fragmentation, soil erosion, geomorphologic hazards, interference with flora and fauna, and visibility. The study concluded that two of the proposed ski areas are located in a highly unsuitable environment, and that the relevant plan provisions should be revised.

Utzinger, J., Wyss, K., Moto, D. D., Yemadji, N., Tanner, M. and Singer, B. H. (2005) 'Assessing health impacts of the Chad-Cameroon petroleum development and pipeline project: Challenges and a way forward', *Environmental Impact Assessment Review*, vol 25, no 1, pp63–93

This article focuses on a large infrastructure development in sub-Saharan Africa – namely, the Chad–Cameroon petroleum development and pipeline project. The main purpose of this paper is to identify and discuss challenges, and to propose a way forward, regarding the assessment of health impacts of the Chad–Cameroon petroleum project. The authors state that although most projects, programmes and policies that undergo EIA also require the consideration of health, relatively few provide adequate appraisals of those impacts. The paper presents a summary of the genesis and actual implementation of the Chad–Cameroon project, develops and applies a guiding framework for health impact assessment, and advances a series of recommendations for broad determinants of health beyond the project's fence line.

3.7.3 Regulatory Impact Assessment (RIA)

Exemplary evaluation question relating to regulatory impact assessment

- What are the possible or probable side effects of (new) regulatory measures? These side effects might cover administrative processes internal to those elaborated upon or they may address societal processes.

3.7.3.1 Elucidation and context

The essence of the method

What?

Regulatory impact assessment (RIA) is an evaluation system, an evaluation method and a product of evaluation. In most Organisation for Economic Co-operation and Development (OECD) countries, it is applied as a method for the systematic assessment of benefits and drawbacks of new or existing legislation for the purpose of enhancing the quality of legislative policy. RIA is also an evaluation method that answers concrete evaluative questions relating to specific legislation. Finally, RIA is a product of evaluation: an RIA is a document in which (in accordance with a fixed pattern) an evaluation is made of the legislation to be assessed.

An RIA requires a structured analysis of the envisaged objectives and the expected positive and negative effects of a drafted piece of legislation, in comparison with alternatives.

In the literature, a distinction is made between a screening RIA and a full RIA (Department of the Taoiseach, 2008). A screening RIA may be described as a brief checklist leading to the collection of a number of contextual data regarding the regulation to be assessed (rationale behind the intervention, objectives of the regulation, choice of instruments) and the available data regarding expected benefits and costs.

A full RIA may be described as a thorough study which, besides providing an indication of a number of important contextual aspects relating to the regulation involved (as in a screening RIA), also fulfils the following requirements:

- a description of the various policy options that can help to achieve the goals;
- an appraisal of the effects of each of these policy options;
- a consultation of the target groups and representatives of groups that may undergo external effects of the various policy options;
- formulation of policy recommendations in favour of the preferred policy option on the basis of the appraisal of effects and public consultation;

- formulation of suggestions for the implementation of policy and the retention of a preferred policy option;
- formulation of recommendations relating to the organization of an *ex post* cost-benefit analysis of the regulation studied.

The screening RIA is 'light' in the sense that it does not require a substantial amount of work on the part of the evaluator. A full RIA is 'heavy' in the sense that it requires an altogether more thorough and extensive approach.

When?

One of the fundamental goals of an RIA is to reduce the unnecessary use of regulation through an examination of the possible use of alternatives. This requires that RIAs must be conducted at an early stage and before a decision to regulate has been taken. This means that it is at least possible to consider the use of alternatives to regulation or lighter forms of regulation even if they are not necessarily considered to be the most appropriate approach in the long run (Department of the Taoiseach, 2008).

Advantages and disadvantages?

RIA has several advantages. RIA:

- enhances insight into the actual situation to which regulation applies;
- detects possible options for attaining the intended policy objectives;
- encourages reflection on expected costs, benefits and effects of policy options;
- enhances the involvement of other authorities and target groups;
- allows one to take prior account of implementation, enforcement and evaluation;
- ensures that the political decision-makers are better informed.

As an evaluation system, RIA also has a number of potential drawbacks:

- In the long term, RIA may degenerate into a formalist procedure.
- RIA may create the illusion of being an objective evaluation, while it may, in fact, be a deliberate strategy to push forward a particular policy option (and not necessarily the most appropriate one). The choice of who should conduct an RIA is therefore of the greatest importance.

Historical context

RIAs were introduced during the 1970s in the US. As a system, RIA was first institutionalized in the UK in 1998. Meanwhile, the approach is also applied in, among other countries, Australia, Canada, Denmark, France, Germany, Mexico and The Netherlands.

Research and evaluation context

RIA belongs to the group of impact assessments and, internationally, is one of the traditional methods for *ex ante* and *ex post* evaluation of policy (i.e. new regulations).

3.7.3.2 Methodology

BOX 3.8 THE FIVE STEPS WITHIN A SCREENING REGULATORY IMPACT ASSESSMENT

1 Description of policy context, objectives and options.
2 Identification of costs, benefits and other impacts of each option.
3 Consultation.
4 Enforcement and compliance.
5 Review.

Steps in RIA

The steps of a screening RIA are summarized in Box 3.8.

Description of policy context, objectives and options

The RIA should begin by describing the policy context: the background to the issue, the particular policy problem or challenge it poses, and the conditions/imperatives for resolving the problem. Once the context has been provided, the objectives of the proposed action should be identified. In other words, what are the regulations or alternative policy tool intended to achieve? It is important here to recognize the difference between general or ultimate objectives and immediate objectives. Both should be included in the RIA. Once the context and objectives have been detailed, the policy options for achieving the objectives must be described. International best practice indicates that the 'do nothing' or 'no policy change' option should be included as an option.

Identification of costs, benefits and other impacts of each option

Once the options have been outlined, the cost, benefits and impacts of these options should be identified and described. For the purpose of the screening RIA, formal cost-benefit analysis (see Section 3.8 'Cost-effectiveness analysis (CEA) and cost-benefit analysis (CBA)') is unnecessary, but, where possible, monetize cost/benefits and impacts and/or quantify them (express them numerically – for example, number/proportion of lives saved, reduction in traffic volumes, etc.). The level of detail included should be proportionate to the significance and likely impact of the proposal.

Consultation

Informal consultation must be conducted as part of a screening RIA. Consultation with key stakeholders should take place as early as possible in the RIA process so that it can feed into the analysis of costs, benefits and impacts.

Enforcement and compliance

Compliance costs will already have been detailed as part of step 2 of the RIA (identification of costs, benefits and other impacts of each option). The RIA should also include specific information as to how enforcement of the regulations is to be achieved. Regulations that are not enforced will not achieve their objectives. A key question that must be addressed within the RIA is whether the regulations are enforceable within the budget and constraints available. Where the answer to this question is no, an alternative policy option must be considered.

Review

The final step in the screening RIA is to identify mechanisms for periodically reviewing the regulations to evaluate the extent to which they are achieving the objectives/intended benefits. Possible review mechanisms include reporting on performance within annual reports, consulting with stakeholders and establishing review groups.

A full RIA should be conducted where the screening RIA suggests that any one of the following applies:

- There will be significant negative impacts on national competitiveness.
- There will be significant negative impacts on the socially excluded or vulnerable groups.
- There will be significant environmental damage.
- The proposals involve a significant policy change in an economic market or will have a significant impact upon competition or consumers.
- The proposals will disproportionately impinge upon the rights of citizens.
- The proposals will impose a disproportionate compliance burden.
- The costs to the exchequer or third parties are significant.

The full RIA is essentially a more detailed version of the screening RIA. A summary of the steps of a full RIA are set out in Box 3.9.

BOX 3.9 THE SEVEN STEPS WITHIN A FULL REGULATORY IMPACT ASSESSMENT

1   Statement of a policy problem and objective.
2   Identification and description of options.
3   Impact analysis, including costs and benefits of each option.
4   Consultation.
5   Enforcement of and compliance for each option.
6   Review.
7   Summary and recommendations.

Statement of policy problem and objective

The statement of the policy problem should follow a similar format to the first step of the screening RIA. Details should be supplied on the background to the issue and why it has to be addressed at this particular time.

Identification and description of options

A full RIA requires a more detailed analysis of options than the screening RIA. Each option should be clearly described and explained. Where an option has a number of components, detail each one.

Impact analysis including costs and benefits of each option

The basic principles outlined for the screening RIA also apply in conducting a full RIA. However, a full RIA involves a more detailed and rigorous analysis of impacts, costs and benefits. In some cases, full cost-benefit analysis will be necessary (see Section 3.8 'Cost-effectiveness analysis (CEA) and cost-benefit analysis (CBA)').

Consultation

Formal (structured) consultation is a compulsory part of a full RIA. This should take place at an early stage in the impact analysis. Formal consultation differs from informal consultation in a number of ways. It is usually based on a written document, it encompasses a wider population and it involves a specific time period for responses. It should be widely publicized through appropriate channels, such as advertisements in the media, on government websites, etc.

Enforcement and compliance for each option

The full RIA should involve a detailed examination of enforcement and compliance issues for each option being considered.

Review

As time goes on, changes in the particular policy area may mean that the regulations become out of date or no longer meet their objectives. Regulations must therefore be reviewed regularly and RIAs should detail the mechanisms by which the regulations/regulatory alternatives will be reviewed. These might include the establishment of new reporting mechanisms, such as dedicated sections on regulations within, for example, annual reports.

Summary and recommendations

International best practice suggests that the final step of an RIA should be a recommendation to proceed with one of the options analysed. In some RIAs, there may be an obvious preferred option and a recommendation will therefore be appropriate. In other policy areas, it may be necessary to reflect other considerations so that the final step should simply be to summarize the pros and cons of each option. The key decision-maker (usually the relevant minister) will then decide which of the options to implement.

References and Examples

Primary and additional references

Baldwin, R. and Cave, M. (1999) *Understanding Regulation: Theory, Strategy and Practice*, Oxford University Press, Oxford, UK

Ballantine, B. and Devonald, B. (2006) 'Modern regulatory impact analysis: The experience of the European Union', *Regulatory Toxicology and Pharmacology*, vol 44, no 1, pp57–68

Cabinet Office (2000) *Good Policy Making: A Guide to Regulatory Impact Assessment*, Cabinet Office, London

Department of the Taoiseach (2008) 'RIA guidelines – how to conduct a regulatory impact analysis', www.betterregulation.ie, accessed 1 March 2008

Kirkpatrick, C. and Parker, D. (2004) 'Regulatory impact assessment and regulatory governance in developing countries', *Public Administration and Development*, vol 24, no 4, pp333–345

OECD (Organisation for Economic Co-operation and Development) (1995) *Recommendation on Improving the Quality of Government Regulation*, OECD, Paris

OECD (2005) 'OECD guiding principles for regulatory quality and performance', www.oecd.org/dataoecd/24/6/34976533.pdf, accessed 1 March 2008

Examples

Wilkinson, D., Monkhouse, C., Herodes, M. and Farmer, A. (2005) *For Better or for Worse? The EU's 'Better Regulation' Agenda and the Environment*, Report by the

Institute for European Environmental Policy (IEEP), www.ieep.eu/publications/
pdfs/2005/for betterorforworse.pdf, accessed 1 March 2008

The European Commission has launched various proposals on improving
EU legislation. What this improvement should imply is still to be discussed. The
IEEP report investigates the wide range of 'beter regulation' initiatives that have
been proposed at the EU level and scrutinizes their implications on the future
direction of EU environmental policy and its effectiveness. The report refers to
many examples of the impact of EU environmental legislation upon the
environmental policy of member states.

Meyer-Ohlendorf, N., Mehling, M. and Neubauer, A. (2006) *Legal Aspects of
User Charges on Global Environmental Goods*, Report Institute for International
and European Environmental Policy, www.umweltbundesamt.de/umweltrecht-e/
index.htm, accessed 1 March 2008

Global environmental goods such as airspace and the oceans can be used by
anyone, with virtually no restrictions and free of charge. The growth in aviation
and shipping is causing a substantial rise in environmental impacts. In order to
counteract this development, the introduction of user charges is investigated. The
study *Legal Aspects of User Charges on Global Environmental Goods*, commissioned
by the German Federal Environment Agency, presents concrete proposals on how
such user charges (e.g. ticket fees and port fees) can be designed within the
framework of international, European and German national law.

3.8 COST-EFFECTIVENESS ANALYSIS (CEA) AND COST-BENEFIT ANALYSIS (CBA)

> *Exemplary evaluation questions relating to cost-effectiveness and cost-benefit analyses*
>
> - What are the costs and effects of various policy alternatives? Which policy alternative is the most suitable, feasible or affordable?
> - Do the costs of the policy weigh its benefits, effects or added value, expressed either in monetary or non-monetary terms?

3.8.1 Elucidation and context

The essence of the two methods

What?

Cost-effectiveness analysis (CEA) and cost-benefit analysis (CBA) are the most commonly applied methods for analysing and assessing the efficacy and/or efficiency of policy interventions. They belong to the economic approach of evaluation research and offer a framework for connecting the costs associated with a policy programme with policy outcomes.

Cost-benefit analysis is a method for determining whether the added value of a project, activity or programme outweighs its cost. In order to reach a conclusion on the desirability of the policy programme, all of its aspects – positive as well as negative – must be expressed in the same unit of measurement. The most commonly applied common unit of measurement is money. In CBA, the benefits of a policy are expressed as a monetary value and compared with the costs (to be) incurred. CBA is also applied to compare the costs and benefits of alternative policy proposals or measures. Occasionally one speaks of 'social cost-benefit analysis'. Unlike in a traditional CBA, a social CBA takes into account a number of social costs and benefits that are not encompassed by the regular market mechanisms (e.g. external costs and benefits). Most environmental goods (such as clean air) fall under this category. In the framework of environmental policy, any CBA is therefore a social CBA. For this reason, one does not make this distinction in the context of environmental policy and one simply tends to speak of CBA.

The main difference between CBA and CEA is that, in the analysis of cost-effectiveness, one does not need to express the cost of the policy intervention in monetary terms. One proceeds on the basis of existing, clear and, as the case may be, measurable policy objectives – for example, the number of human lives that a policy has saved. Subsequently, the cost is calculated that is associated with achieving this objective. In principle, in CEA, one proposes the policy alternative that achieves the policy objective at the lowest cost.

When?

CEA and CBA can be used either as methods for weighing up policy alternatives against each other or to evaluate ongoing policy programmes.

In the policy planning phase, CEA and CBA can be conducted *ex ante* on the basis of estimations or anticipated costs and benefits. In this instance, the central question is which policy alternative to choose. The answer of the CBA is fourfold. First and foremost, one may opt for the alternative where the relation between costs and benefits is the most favourable. In the second instance, one may opt for the zero alternative (i.e. do nothing) in cases where the costs outweigh the benefits regardless of which alternative one considers. Third, one may have determined beforehand that the costs should not exceed a certain level. In such a case, the cost is used as a veto criterion. Fourth, the plausibility of the outcome should not become uncertain.

CBA can also be applied as a form of *ex post* or *ex nunc* programme evaluation. CBA is, in this context, often used for gaining insight into the price tag of a programme or in order to determine whether financial efforts have contributed to achieving the policy objectives and/or the creation of societal benefits (Stufflebeam, 2001, p31).

A number of conditions need to be fulfilled in order to be able to conduct a CBA or CEA:

- The possibility of conducting a CBA depends upon whether or not costs and benefits can be expressed quantitatively and in monetary terms. If this is not the case, then one speaks of imponderabilia. Examples that come to mind are criteria such as equity, impact upon sustainable development and political acceptability.
- The success of CEA and CBA will also depend upon the availability of administrative data and the willingness of the administration to allow access to and to analyse the data.

Advantages and disadvantages?

One of the disadvantages of CBA is that the allocation of costs and benefits over different actors is not incorporated within the analysis. A public authority will nevertheless need to take this into account: who stands to benefit from the policy programme and who will foot the bill? In this context, we also speak of the distributive effects of policy. In some cases, one may opt for weighting of certain costs and benefits. For example, one may decide that costs to the poor should be attributed greater weight than costs to the rich.

Furthermore, ethical objections to CBA are sometimes raised because of the monetization of certain benefits, such as the value of a human life, the value of preserving a particular kind of insect, etc. This at once brings us to an advantage of CEA: benefits are expressed in other than monetary terms.

On the other hand, a CEA has the disadvantage that one can only compare policy alternatives with the same objectives. CBA does not have this disadvantage: as long as costs and benefits are translatable into a monetary value, all conceivable alternatives can be compared, even if they differ in terms of objectives or belong to different policy domains.

Historical context

The notion of 'economic accounting' was introduced during the mid 19th century by the French engineer Jules Dupuit. Later, the British economist Alfred Marshall formulated some of the concepts that would come to constitute the foundation of CBA. The impetus for the practical development of CBA was provided by the US Federal Navigation Act of 1936. This act required that the US Corps of Engineers execute projects for improving the waterway when the total benefits of a project outweighed its costs. This meant that the engineers of the corps had to devise a systematic method for measuring and comparing such costs and benefits. They did this without much help from economists. It was not until 20 years later, during the 1950s, that economists set out in search of a rigorous, consistent set of methods to analyse and assess the costs and benefits of a project. Today, the basic principles of CBA are widely accepted.

Research and evaluation context

CBA is an economic measurement model that can be used for *ex ante* and *ex post* policy evaluations. CEA, on the other hand, is a truly scientific policy evaluation method.

Ex ante CBA is useful for policy measures that, once they have been taken, are hard to undo or for policy measures that require a substantial implementation effort. Decisions on the application of technology in healthcare and environmental policy are often preceded by CBA because they are capital intensive.

Generally speaking, CBA is more broadly applicable than CEA. Whereas CBA can be used in the context of projects and activities (e.g. the construction of a bridge), as well as policy programmes, CEA is used primarily for comparison of alternatives in the outlining of future policy.

Both CBA and CEA bear certain resemblances to impact assessment. The main difference between CBA and impact assessment (see Section 3.7) is that the latter method does not involve expressing all elements in a common unit of measurement (e.g. Euros). The difference between CEA and impact assessment is that impact assessment does not necessarily try to optimize the situation in order to minimize cost (Tietenberg, 2005).

3.8.2 Methodology

Steps in CBA and CEA

There is a logical sequence of steps to be taken in CEA and CBA. These steps are represented schematically in Figure 3.2.

The first step entails an investigation and assessment of the policy problem, its context and background (step 1). Subsequently, the policy objectives are analysed (step 2) and constraints on policy action are examined and documented (step 3). Examples of such constraints are limitations on staff numbers or

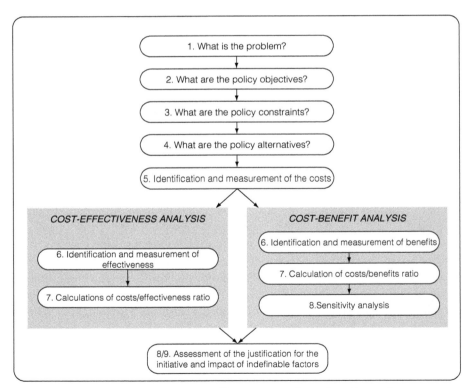

Figure 3.2   *Steps in cost-effectiveness and cost-benefit analysis*

Source: adapted from Council of Australian Governments (2004)

financial resources. Then, the policy options are considered (step 4), including the zero alternative (i.e. the option not to take policy action). In the fifth step, the cost of (possible) policy action is examined and calculated.

Thus far, the sequence of steps in CEA and CBA are identical. But they subsequently diverge:

- In the case of CEA, step 6 consists of analysing the impact of the policy initiative: the policy effects are identified and quantified (in non-monetary terms). In the seventh step, the ratio is calculated of the costs and the policy effects. Finally, the evaluator makes an assessment of the justifiability of the (proposed) policy initiative. The evaluator should also check that no relevant factors have been overlooked.
- In the case of CBA, step 6 always involves identifying the benefits of the policy intervention and their quantification in monetary value. In step 7, the ratio between costs and benefits is calculated. Next, in step 8, the evaluator is required to carry out a sensitivity analysis. This implies that one should examine the impact of estimation errors on the results of the CBA. A 'sensitivity analysis' encompasses:
  1. substitution of the most pessimistic estimates and a recalculation; and
  2. an assessment of the sensitivity of the cost-benefit model applied.

The latter implies that one should ascertain to what extent the analysis is affected if one changes a single variable in the model. CBA is also concluded with an assessment of the justification of the (proposed) policy action and a check on whether undefined variables may have impacted upon the cost-benefit model.

Remarks

When conducting a CEA or CBA, special attention should be paid to a number of aspects:

- One must take into account variations in monetary value over time. As a result of fluctuations in supply and demand, or due inflation, the value attributed to costs and benefits may change. CEA and CBA must discount such fluctuations in the calculations. This is done by recalculating all costs and benefits on the basis of the net present value. However, there is no agreement in the literature on how precisely one should proceed.
- In CEAs and CBAs, one makes certain assumptions about the relationship between incurring costs and achieving benefits. However, one needs to ascertain that the assumptions by the evaluator and those by the policy-makers correspond, as well as whether they are empirically verifiable.

References and Examples

Primary and additional references

Angelsen, A. and Sumaila, U. R. (1995) *Hard Methods for Soft Policies: Environmental and Social Cost-Benefit Analysis*, Michelsen Institute, Bergen, Norway

Council of Australian Governments (2004) *Principles and Guidelines for National Standard Setting and Regulatory Action by Ministerial Councils and Standard-Setting Bodies – Report COAG*, www.coag.gov.au/meetings/250604/coagpg04.pdf, accessed 1 March 2008

Gramlich, E. M. (1990) *A Guide to Benefit-Cost Analysis*, 2nd edition, Prentice Hall, New York, NY

Hanley, N. and Spash, C. L. (1993) *Cost-Benefit Analysis and the Environment*, Edward Elgar Publishing Limited, Aldershot, UK

Johansson, P. O. (1993) *Cost-Benefit Analysis of Environmental Change*, Cambridge University Press, Cambridge, UK

Kee, J. E. (2004) 'Cost-effectiveness and cost-benefit analysis', in J. S. Wholey, H. P. Hatry and K. E. Newcomer (eds) *Handbook of Practical Program Evaluation*, 2nd edition, Jossey-Bass, San Francisco, CA

Kuik, O. J., Oosterhuis, F. H., Jansen, H. M. A., Holm, K. and Ewers, H. J. (1992) *Assessment of Benefits of Environmental Measures*, Graham and Trotman, London

Levin, H. M. and McEwan, P. C. (2000) *Cost-Effectiveness Analysis: Methods and Applications*, 2nd edition, Sage, Thousand Oaks, CA

Mishan, E. J. (1988) *Cost-Benefit Analysis*, 4th edition, Unwin Hyman, London

Stufflebeam, D. L. (2001) 'Evaluation models', *New Directions for Evaluation*, no 89

Tietenberg, T. (2005) *Environmental and Natural Resource Economics*, 7th edition, Addison Wesley, Boston, MA

Watkins, T. (undated) 'Introduction to cost-benefit analysis', www2.sjsu.edu/faculty/Watkins/cba.htm, accessed 1 March 2008

Examples

Georgiou, S. and Bateman, I. (2005) 'Revision of the EU bathing water directive: Economic costs and benefits', *Marine Pollution Bulletin*, vol 50, no 4, pp430–438

The European Union (EU) Bathing Water Directive of 1976 sets out standards for designated bathing waters that should be complied with by all member states. Intervening advances in pollution science, related technology and managerial expertise have allowed the European Commission to consider revision of EU environmental legislation where appropriate. As a result, a number of revisions to the 1976 Directive have been proposed. This paper considers these revisions in terms of the economic costs and benefits associated with any change in policy. The focus is on the public's willingness to pay for a revised directive and the consequent public health benefits afforded to individuals and society. These economic benefits are compared to the costs of implementing changes to bring bathing waters up to the required standard.

Kishimoto, A., Kishimoto, A., Oka, T., Yoshida, K. and Nakanishi, J. (2001) 'Cost effectiveness of reducing dioxin emissions from municipal solid waste incinerators in Japan', *Environmental Science and Technology*, vol 35, no 14, pp2861–2866

The Japanese national government has set an emission standard for dioxins to reduce dioxin exposure levels. In this study, a cost-effectiveness analysis was carried out regarding measures for reducing dioxin emissions of municipal solid waste incinerators. The authors calculated the cost per life-year saved. It was estimated to be 7.9 million yen for emergency measures and 150 million yen for long-term measures.

3.9 LOGFRAME METHOD/LOGICAL FRAMEWORK APPROACH (LFA)

Exemplary evaluation questions relating to the logical framework approach

- Does the formulation of the policy objectives pay sufficient attention to monitoring and evaluating the policy performances at a later stage?
- Has one anticipated an *ex post* policy evaluation, including the data availability needed (see Chapter 2)?

3.9.1 Elucidation and context

The essence of the method

What?

The logical framework approach (LFA) is essentially a methodology for substantiating and evaluating the plans for specific policy projects. LFA may be helpful in answering the following questions:

- Why are we engaging in this project?
- What results are we expecting (in relation to the investment made in terms of manpower and finances)?
- Who stands to benefit from the project?
- What are the needs and priorities of the members of the target group?
- How will the results of the project be measured?

In the literature, the approach is regarded as a solid instrument that can be of particular assistance to planners and other policy-makers in the following tasks:

- project development (by analysing the existing situation);
- determining the logical coherence between objectives and means deployed;
- identifying potential risks;
- specifying how policy output and outcome should be monitored and evaluated;
- presenting a project summary in a standard format;
- monitoring and following up the project implementation.

The last point illustrates how LFA, besides offering a technique for project planning, also provides a starting point for evaluating policy projects.

The result of applying the approach can be represented in a matrix (a so-called logframe) summarizing the objectives of the project, the project organization, the basic assumptions behind the project, and the strategy for following up on and evaluating the project output and outcome. The term logframe, or logical framework, refers to the logical connections that planners make between the policy objective and available resources.

Participation by interested parties is an important ingredient of LFA. Indeed, LFA can be used to involve stakeholders in setting strategic goals, composing a (causally connected) chain of expected policy products, identifying underlying assumptions and possible risks, and selecting suitable indicators for measuring policy performances. Participation is deemed to be important because it prevents LFA from leading to policy projects that only work on paper. Involving the stakeholders is seen as a necessary reality check.

When?
While LFA can be applied at all stages of the policy cycle of a specific project or programme, it is particularly suitable during policy programme design. After all, it provides assistance in identifying policy needs, in preparing the project content and in evaluating the draft projects. The approach is, however, also useful in the follow up of the project implementation and in its monitoring/evaluation.

Advantages and disadvantages?
The approach offers the following advantages:

- LFA has the potential to summarize complex projects clearly and comprehensibly on just one or two sheets of paper.
- In the early stage of project planning, LFA can be applied to test the relevance and utility of project ideas.
- In part because of the participatory approach, LFA allows one to draw up plans that are executable, taking into account the risks and dangers involved in project implementation.
- Logframes (the matrices) can provide a basis for contracts in which agreements are made about what should be delivered when the project is implemented.
- As the project is implemented, a logframe may serve as a point of reference in the design of operational plans, and in the setting of deadlines, budgets, etc.
- Logframes provide indicators and measures on the basis of which the progress of the project and goal attainment can be determined.

For these and other reasons, LFA is a well-known and broadly accepted methodology. Still, the approach has a number of disadvantages:

- LFA focuses too much on problems and leaves little room for debate on opportunities and possibilities.

Table 3.2 *Logframe*

	Assumptions underlying the project (1)	Indicators for measuring performances (2)
Strategic objective	What is the strategic objective of the project?	Which indicators are related to the general objective of the project?
Operational objective of the project	What are the specific objectives connected with the project?	Which quantitative or qualitative indicators measure whether the specific project objectives are achieved (and to what extent)?
Expected results	Which concrete output is required in order to attain the specific objectives? Which effects and benefits does the project envisage? Which improvements or changes will the project give rise to?	Which indicators measure whether (and to what extent) the project will achieve the envisaged objectives and effects?
Activities	What are the main activities that need to be carried out and in which order should they be executed in order to attain the expected results?	Which means are required in order to carry out these activities (e.g. personnel, equipment, training, research, etc.)?

Source: based on AusAid (2000)

- If LFA is applied too strictly, it will lead to blueprint planning (a rather inflexible approach to project planning).
- Little attention is paid to issues of uncertainty, while it is important in the development and management of projects that learning should be stimulated and flexibility should be incorporated in the face of changing circumstances.
- There is a danger that the logframe is filled up with ill-considered information regarding objectives and resources, while the purpose is to provide a solid foundation for projects.
- LFA does not allow one to draw conclusions with regard to any causal relationship between the project and whether or not the policy objectives are achieved.

Historical context

The logical framework approach was introduced in the 1960s by the US Defence Department and was subsequently developed further by the

Information sources (3)	Contextual assumptions (4)
Which information sources can be used for these indicators?	
Which information sources are available for these indicators? How can these sources be complemented? Which methods are to be used to collect the data?	Which factors and conditions (that are not under the project manager's direct control) are necessary in order to attain the specific project objectives? Which risks should be taken into account?
Which information sources are available for these indicators?	Which external factors and conditions must be fulfilled in order to achieve the expected output and results (in time)?
Which information sources may be relied on to monitor project progress?	Which conditions need to be fulfilled before the project gets under way? Which preconditions (beyond the control of the project manager) must be satisfied in order to be able to carry out the planned activities?

US Agency for International Development (USAID). Since its introduction, the approach has evolved from a simple framework for moulding project objectives into a process-oriented methodology where a whole range of interested parties may be involved in the design, evaluation and adjustment of the project.

Research and evaluation context

The logframe approach belongs to the tradition of results-oriented evaluation methods. The distinguishing feature of these methods is that first the objectives of the policy action are determined, after which the evaluation focuses on whether or not these objectives are attained. The information that is provided by this type of evaluation study is used to reformulate the objectives. LFA also ties in with the tradition of *management-oriented approaches*, which are intended to result in evaluations that can help policy-makers in decision-making.

3.9.2 Methodology

Steps in the logframe method

The application of the logical framework approach involves six steps, as outlined in Box 3.10.

As we have previously pointed out, an LFA yields a matrix (or *logframe*). This matrix can be read horizontally as well as vertically. The 'vertical logic' indicates which assumptions one has in relation to the project (column 1) and which factors and (pre)conditions beyond the control of the project managers are relevant to the project (column 4). The 'horizontal logic' concerns the question of how policy performances within the framework of the project should be measured (column 2) and how these measurements should be substantiated (column 3). The 'horizontal logic' constitutes the foundation for monitoring and evaluating the project.

It is normal for the initial *logframe* of the project to be adapted during the project implementation. These adaptations demonstrate that, as the project unfolds, those involved are gaining better insight into cause and effect, problem and solution.

Remarks

LFA requires the deployment of a number of analysis techniques: problem analyses, risk assessments, goal trees, stakeholder analyses, etc.

BOX 3.10 THE SIX STEPS WITHIN THE LOGICAL FRAMEWORK APPROACH

1   Determination of the objectives and scope of the project.
2   Agreement on the organizational framework in which the project is to be prepared, the procedural rules in the design of the project and the conceptual definitions (see also Section 4.11 'Utilization-focused evaluation (U-FE)').
3   A detailed situational analysis.
4   Development of a project strategy: setting of a hierarchy of objectives (see also Section 3.2 'Programme theory evaluation') and agreeing on the implementation of the project – more specifically, the resources to be deployed.
5   Specification of the assumptions and risks associated with the strategy chosen; analysis of these assumptions and risks; and adjustment to the project design (if assumptions are proven wrong or if the risks are too great).
6   Development of a framework for project monitoring and evaluation.

References and Examples

Primary and additional references

AusAID (2000) 'AusGUIDElines 1 the logical framework approach', www.school netafrica.net/fileadmin/1MillionPCsTraining/Resources/Module%206/ausgui de lines-1.pdf, accessed 1 March 2008

CIDA (Canadian International Development Agency) (1985) *Guide for the Use of the Logical Framework Approach in the Management and Evaluation of CIDA's International Development Projects*, CIDA, Gatineau, Canada

Danida (1995) *Logical Framework Approach: A Flexible Tool for Participatory Development*, Royal Danish Ministry for Foreign Affairs, Denmark

European Commission (1993) *Project Cycle Management*, European Directorate-General for Development, Brussels, Belgium

European Commission (2001) *Manual Project Cycle Management*, Europe Aid Co-operation Office, Brussels, Belgium, http://ec.europa.eu/echo/pdf_files/partnership/guidelines/project_cycle_mngmt_en.pdf, accessed 1 March 2008

NORAD (Norwegian Agency for Development Cooperation) (1999) *The Logical Framework Approach: Handbook for Objectives-Oriented Planning*, 4th edition, NORAD, Oslo, Norway, www.norad.no/default.asp?V_ITEM_ID=1069, accessed 1 March 2008

SIDA (Swedish Agency for International Development Cooperation) (1996) *Guidelines for the Application of the Logical Framework Approach in Project Cycle Management*, SIDA, Stockholm, Sweden

SIDA (2004) *The Logical Framework Approach: A Summary of the Theory behind the LFA Method*, SIDA, Stockholm, Sweden, www.sida.se (publikationer, the logical framework approach), accessed 1 March 2008

World Bank (1996) *Performance Monitoring Indicators: A Handbook for Task Managers*, World Bank, Washington, DC, www.worldbank.org/html/opr/pmi/maintxt.html, accessed 1 March 2008

Examples

Johnson, C. (2007) 'Impacts of prefabricated temporary housing after disasters: 1999 earthquakes in Turkey', *Habitat International*, vol 31, no 1, pp36–52

This article discusses temporary housing programmes and the problems they tend to provoke, such as high costs and undesirable impacts upon the urban environment. Using the logical framework approach, a case study is made of the temporary housing programme for the 1999 earthquakes in Turkey. It is found that unwanted effects can be reduced through proper facilities management, reuse of units, and initial application of unit designs that are easy to dismantle.

Eckerman, I. (2005) 'The Bhopal gas leak: Analyses of causes and consequences by three different models', *Journal of Loss Prevention in the Process Industries*, vol 18, no 4–6, pp213–217

The 1984 Bhopal gas leak in India was the largest chemical industrial accident ever. This article tests Haddon's and Berger's models for injury analysis, and the project planning tool logical framework approach. The author states that the three models give somewhat different images of the process of the accident. She stresses that using different models can highlight different aspects.

3.10 MULTI-CRITERIA ANALYSIS (MCA)

Exemplary evaluation questions relating to multi-criteria analysis

- Which policy strategy should one opt for if several alternatives present themselves?
- Which policy strategy is the most desirable, feasible or affordable, given a specific set of criteria?

3.10.1 Elucidation and context

The essence of the method

What?

Multi-criteria analysis (MCA) is a method for weighing up alternative policy action against each other in order to arrive at the 'best' alternative in a complex policy context. Unlike cost-benefit analysis (p°°), the effects are not expressed in monetary terms, but in measurement units that are determined by the nature of the effect (e.g. the reduction of greenhouse gas emissions is expressed in carbon dioxide equivalents).

Multi-criteria analysis tries to incorporate all (conflicting) criteria simultaneously within the analysis. In MCA, the preference(s) and priorities of the policy-makers are incorporated within the decision model. Consequently, MCA is typically a subjective evaluation.

When?

Multi-criteria analysis is typically applied in the policy formation phase: it is a method that allows one to compare various alternatives during the planning phase with different, complex objectives and to arrive at a well-founded decision. In other words, MCA is an example of an *ex ante* evaluation method.

Multi-criteria analysis is a suitable alternative if CBA and CEA are impossible (due to excessive complexity or inadequate data) or deemed inappropriate (for ethical reasons or otherwise).

Advantages and disadvantages?

The main advantage of MCA is that it can be applied in increasingly more complex situations than CBA. Even if information is incomparable (how, for example, does one compare the objectives of policy-makers with the opinions of interest groups?) and if objectives conflict, the method can be applied.

Central to the methodology is the significance that the policy-maker attaches to specific criteria. This is, at once, a strength and a weakness:

- The advantages are that MCA allows one to weigh up options in situations where there is a lack of objective and quantitative measures for making policy decisions; MCA therefore scores higher in terms of policy relevance than most other, merely academic, methods.
- The disadvantage is that the scores that policy makers attribute (see the following sub-section 'Steps in classical MCA' in Section 3.10.2) are not always based on clearly defined measures and occasionally lack transparency.

The (Dutch) commission on environmental impact assessment further identifies the following disadvantages:

- Because of the great complexity and the technical nature of most components of an MCA, the method is inaccessible to non-experts.
- The choices in the assignment of weights to the various criteria must be communicated transparently; otherwise, one creates room for manipulation.
- Since there is no standard method for attributing weights, weighting is inevitably debatable.

Historical context

Since MCA is not a single method but a group of methods (see 'Steps in classical MCA' in Section 3.10.2), there is no common history. Most methods were developed during the 1970s and 1980s.

Research and evaluation context

Like CBA, MCA can be applied in terms of choices at the project level, as well as in the domain of policy-making. The difference is that in the case of CBA, all costs and benefits are expressed in monetary values. In cases where it is important that the values of the policy makers are incorporated within the evaluation, MCA is the only feasible methodology.

3.10.2 Methodology

Steps in classical MCA

In an MCA, one typically weighs up different policy options. This happens on the basis of a number of criteria against which each alternative is tested. Usually, a score is attributed to a criterion in order to allow comparison.

A typical MCA problem consists of a set of policy options (possibly policy actions) that need to be tested against a fixed set of criteria. Thus, the policy question is translated into a large matrix where each alternative is assessed for each criterion. This matrix is sometimes also referred to as the evaluation table (Janssen and Munda, 2002, p838). A score is assigned to each cell of the matrix on the basis of a weighting factor that represents the importance that the policy-maker attaches to the criterion relative to the other criteria. In this way, one incorporates the policy priorities within the assessment. Subsequently, a ranking is drawn up of the various alternatives on the basis of their score for the various criteria.

The effects and weights may be entirely quantitative, entirely qualitative or a combination of the two. Depending upon the case to be evaluated, one will have to apply a different method. Without claiming to be exhaustive, we will consider some important methods for the purpose of MCA.

Weighted summation

In this simple method, the various criterion scores are multiplied by the criterion weights; subsequently, one adds up the scores per alternative, resulting in a unique overall score for each option. On this basis, a ranking is made.

This method can only be applied to quantitative criterion scores.

The goals achievement matrix method (GAM)

Again, the aim is to arrive at a ranking of alternatives. A matrix is drawn up containing two dimensions: goals and alternatives. The principle is that the costs and benefits of various alternatives are linked to explicit goals. For each goal, a cost-benefit account is drawn up that expresses to what extent the goal is achieved.

This method also involves weighting.

Concordance analysis

In this method, the score of each criterion is compared to the score of two alternatives. The perspective is therefore somewhat different than in most other methods: usually one compares the scores of the alternatives on different criteria; here, one considers, per criterion, which alternatives score well (or better) and which do not. This allows one to eliminate a number of alternatives early on – for example, by introducing certain thresholds for a particular criterion: if the alternative attains a score under the threshold, it is rejected.

In a subsequent phase, a more in-depth analysis is carried out and a so-called 'concordance group' is formed, and the analysis shifts to the attribution of scores to the various alternatives (on the basis of information obtained in the previous phase). In this way, an alternative can be selected.

Permutation method

For each criterion, one draws up a ranking. On the basis of the weights and indices, a definitive ranking is made that corresponds most closely with the appreciation of the various criteria. The main drawback of this method is that, depending upon the number of alternatives, one may need powerful software to make all of the necessary calculations.

Regime method

In this method, for each criterion, one compares the scores of two alternatives. The method can be used with quantitative as well as qualitative scores. In the first case, it is always possible to draw up a full ranking of alternatives, while in the second case it is not. The method allows a combination of quantitative and qualitative scores, although certain information will then be lost.

Evamix method

The Evamix method starts from a comprehensive overview of (presumed) effects, which are represented qualitatively as well as quantitatively. Subsequently, for the quantitative and the qualitative effects, separately, one compares with a pair of alternatives (as in the concordance method). This yields 'dominance scores' for both groups of effects. Next, the two sets of scores need to be standardized so that they can be compared.

The main strength of this method is that it is most suitable for an analysis where some effects are qualitative and others quantitative in nature. The main weakness is, again, that it involves complex calculations, necessitating computer software.

References and Examples

Primary and additional references

Dodgson, J., Dodgson, J., Spackman, M., Pearman, A. D. and Phillips, L. D. (2000) *Multi-Criteria Analysis: A Manual*, Department of the Environment, Transport and Regions, London, www.communities.gov.uk/documents/corporate/pdf/146868, accessed 1 March 2008

Janssen, R. and Munda, G. (2002) 'Multi-criteria methods for quantitative, qualitative and fuzzy evaluation problems', in J. C. J. M. Van Den Bergh (ed) *Handbook of Environmental and Resource Economics*, Edward Elgar, Cheltenham, UK, pp831–854

Tietenberg, T. (2005) *Environmental and Natural Resource Economics*, 7th edition, Addison Wesley, Boston, MA

Examples

Phillips, L. and Stock, A. (2003) *Use of Multi-Criteria Analysis in Air Quality Policy: A Report Prepared for the Department for Environment, Food and Rural Affairs*, London

In 2002, the UK Department for Environment, Food and Rural Affairs and the UK Environment Agency decided that they wanted to learn more about multi-criteria analysis and how it might inform the British Air Quality Strategy (AQS) work. This was prompted, in part, by the difficulty in cost-benefit analysis of placing a monetary value on the health and non-health benefits of reductions in air pollution. A pilot study was designed based on two policy areas within the AQS to explore the application of multi-criteria analysis (MCA) techniques during the appraisal of policy options. This report is the final summary of the pilot study.

Janssen, R. and Padilla, J. E. (1996) *Valuation and Evaluation of Management Alternatives for the Pagbilao Mangrove Forest*, CREED Working Paper Series no 9, International Institute for Environment and Development, London, and Institute for Environmental Studies, Vrije Universiteit Amsterdam, The Netherlands, www.prem-online.org/archive/ 17/doc/creed09e.pdf, accessed 1 March 2008

This study evaluated the different management alternatives for the Pagbilao mangroves in the Philippines, looking at various combinations of preservation, subsistence and commercial forestry, silviculture and aquaculture. It carried out a multi-criteria analysis, combining economic, ecological and social information in order to weigh up the relative desirability of different management options. It analysed these different criteria according to the perspectives and objectives of the different types of decision-makers involved in mangrove management, including fishpond owners, local government, national governments and donor agencies.

Hill, G. W. and Crabtree, J. R. (no date) *Applying Concepts of Sustainable Development to Project Evaluation: Ex Post Evaluation of Environmental Projects Funded through EU Structural Funds*, Macaulay Land Use Research Institute, Aberdeen, UK

In the UK for the period of 1994 to 1999, a broad range of environmental projects were given financial support through the European Agriculture Guidance and Guarantee Fund. This paper is concerned with the *ex post* evaluation of these projects set within a sustainable development framework. A multi-criteria analysis was made in order to identify project types or characteristics that offered the greatest return on exchequer investment. The paper concludes that despite the difficulties of defining sustainable development, it is possible to improve the basis for future project selection in order to maximize the returns on environmental investments.

3.11 REALISTIC EVALUATION

Exemplary evaluation questions relating to realistic evaluation

- Does a certain policy have a positive or a negative impact upon societal processes, either within the environmental field or upon adjacent fields, and with which consequences?
- Is there a causal relationship between the policy intervention and the observed effect?

3.11.1 Elucidation and context

The essence of the method

What?

Realistic evaluation (RE) is a method for evaluating the effects of policy. The basic assumption underlying the method is that effects are the product of the interaction between a mechanism and its context. The method is described in Pawson and Tilley (2003). RE is based on the concept of 'generative causation'. With this concept, Pawson and Tilley distance themselves from two other approaches to causality:

1   The traditional approach where, in the social sciences at least, causation is established through serial observation. One starts from the assumption that causality as such cannot be observed (it is external); but it may be determined through a series of observations (e.g. experiments) that allow the researcher to distinguish causation from coincidence.

2   In the second approach, it is asserted that causality may exist as a perception in the mind of the researcher. Here, trust in the expertise of the researcher is central. It is therefore impossible to produce conclusive proof that the causal claim holds.

In the generative (natural scientific) approach to causality, it is assumed that there is an internal explanatory dimension to causality. By adopting this point of view, the question of causality is perceived in a more ambitious and less simplistic way.

In realistic evaluation, the internal explanatory dimension occupies a central position and is considered in a policy context. Pawson and Tilley (2003) speak of *mechanisms* that determine the internal functioning. This approach does not accept the existence of a *black box*. By unravelling the mechanism of interaction between policy and context, RE attempts to lay bare the relationship between policy and effect.

It should be noted here that RE explains the mechanism in a policy programme context. This implies that the context in which the mechanism manifests itself is a co-determining factor of the policy effect. In other words, the effect of a policy is explained through an analysis of the functioning of that policy within the policy context.

When?

RE is applied to answer evaluative questions regarding policy programme effectiveness. This implies that it is primarily an *ex post* approach (i.e. after the policy has been implemented).

Advantages and disadvantages?

The main advantage of realistic evaluation is that the method opens the door for explanatory (generative) causation. It enables the evaluator to open the black box further than is the case with more orthodox evaluation methods such as experimentation (see Section 3.4 'Experiment and quasi-experiment').

There are, however, at least two disadvantages:

1   RE creates a false impression of certainty. There is a danger that, once an explanatory mechanism has been unravelled (in conjunction with a context), causation will be considered proven. However, it will quickly become apparent in practice that, after having unravelled one mechanism, others will also need unravelling. The more mechanisms the evaluator is able to explain, the better he or she will be able to interpret causation. It is, however, exceptional for all underlying mechanisms of a policy programme to be uncovered: there will always remain some unopened black boxes.
2   RE does not allow one to generalize findings. Since the context is regarded as an important explanatory factor, generalization of findings is only possible if the context remains unchanged. As policy contexts usually differ from one another, the possibilities for generalization are very limited indeed.

Historical context

Realistic evaluation builds on the success of realism as a philosophy of science (Pawson and Tilley, 2003, p55). Realism is the golden mean between two extremes: positivism and relativism. Positivism is based on the assumption that basic laws exist, while relativism rejects this notion and argues that no knowledge is absolute. Realism emerged during the early 1970s. It first gained a foothold in the natural sciences. By the end of the 1970s, and particularly during the early 1980s, realism also gained in popularity among social scientists.

Research and evaluation context

According to Pawson and Tilley (2003), the founders of the method, RE is a good alternative to experimentation and qualitative research. They argue that experiments cannot explain the (causal) relationship between policy and effect, while RE can. Still according to Pawson and Tilley (2003), qualitative methods, on the other hand, offer inadequate proof of the causal relationship between policy and effect. Realistic evaluation is more effective in this respect.

3.11.2 Methodology

Steps in realistic evaluation

Realistic evaluation involves the following steps (Pawson and Tilley, 2003):

1   formulation of a theory;
2   formulation of hypotheses;
3   testing of hypotheses on the basis of observations;
4   explaining the functioning of policy.

Formulation of a theory

Here, a theory is understood to mean a comparatively unordered collection of explanations for the (presumably causal) relationship between a policy programme and an effect. Mechanisms and the context are a part of the theory.

Formulation of hypotheses

These hypotheses indicate under which circumstances policy may or may not work and for whom. In fact, the hypotheses are more specifically formulated assumptions regarding the explanations for the relationship between policy and effect.

Testing of hypotheses on the basis of observations

These observations are made in the context of multi-method data collection and analysis. Possible strategies for data collection are quantitative and qualitative methods; longitudinal or cross-sectional research; surveys or participatory observation; etc. The choice for a particular research strategy depends upon the hypotheses that are being studied. Kazi (2003, p32) asserts that, in practice, the choice of method may also depend upon the preference of the evaluator.

Explaining the functioning of policy

In the classical evaluation logic, this is the phase in which one tries to generalize findings. Realistic evaluation, however, does not aspire to uncover absolute basic laws that apply regardless of the situation. RE does have the ambition to discover what has worked for whom and under which conditions.

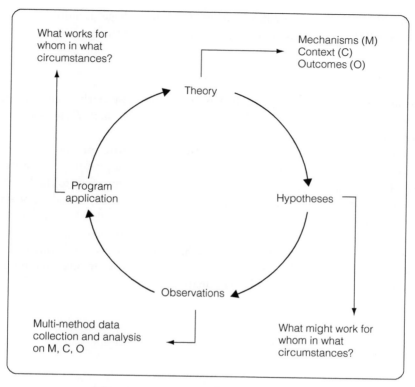

Figure 3.3 *Steps in realistic evaluation*

Source: Pawson and Tilley (2003, p85), reproduced with permission of the authors and publisher

Schematically, the application of the method may be represented as depicted in Figure 3.3.

The realistic evaluation procedure is represented as a circle in order to emphasize that the conclusions drawn in step 4 (i.e. explaining the functioning of policy) provide a new input for step 1 (formulation of a theory). The research results either confirm or refute the theory developed in step 1. In the latter case, the research results provide input for a reformulation of the theory.

References and Examples

Primary and additional references

Kazi, M. (2003) *Realist Evaluation in Practice*, Sage, London

Lawson, T. (1998) 'Economic science without experimentation/abstraction', in M. Archer, R. Bhaskar, A. Collier, T. Lawson and A. Norrie (eds) *Critical Realism: Essential Readings*, Routledge, London

Pawson, R. and Tilley, N. (2003) *Realistic Evaluation*, Sage, London
Sayer, A. (2000) *Realism and Social Science*, Sage, London

Example

Patavalis, D. and Aravossis, K. (2004) 'An evaluation approach to environmental program and project planning', *Water, Air and Soil Pollution: Focus*, vol 4, no 4, pp421–431

This paper presents the incorporation of realistic practice within the formulation of evaluation methodology in environmental planning. The approach is based on the principles of realistic evaluation. Its commitment to the belief that evaluation research depends upon the investigation of causal explanation underlines the fact that environmental interventions are closely connected with and affect the social world. In this way, the social dimension in environmental interventions is enhanced and a more sophisticated perspective is introduced in the evaluation process. Realistic evaluation offers environmental planning and development an actual practice into evaluation.

4

Approaches for Designing
Evaluation Research

Whereas Chapter 3 introduced some classic, well-elaborated upon and tested policy evaluation methods, this chapter focuses on rather different approaches. Grouping them under the heading of 'Approaches to evaluation research design' may seem rather vague and not entirely free of risk. However, despite their obvious differences, the approaches presented here have in common that they essentially try to answer two questions:

1   Can we, in some way or another, mobilize and involve knowledge and expertise that is highly relevant to evaluations and yet is absent from the more classic methods? There may, for example, be approaches that aim to actively involve disagreeing experts and to purposely exploit their divergent opinions or any contradictions between them; they may aim to involve and empower laypeople so that they can participate in the evaluative process on an equal footing with experts and more powerful stakeholders. Or they may even go so far as to present participants' divergent views as alternative criteria for evaluation and/or deliberately build on them with a view to organizing a process of mutual learning and deliberation. In other words, we are concerned here with approaches that adopt an alternative perspective on knowledge input in policy evaluation.
2   How can we enhance the actual utilization and implementation of outcomes, insights and lessons drawn from the evaluative process? This second question relates, perhaps not surprisingly, to the output of evaluative knowledge. One of the approaches presented below boldly claims to be 'utilization focused', while others merely aim to maximize the benefits from, and responses to, policy evaluation by a variety of methods.

Finally, and with relevance to these two questions, it is important that one should assess the evaluability of a given policy (sub)field prior to committing to the evaluative process.

The approaches are listed as follows:

1 advocate–adversary evaluation;
2 context, input, process and product evaluation (CIPP) model;
3 connoisseurship and criticism;
4 constructivist evaluation;
5 deliberative democratic evaluation;
6 empowerment evaluation;
7 evaluability assessment;
8 meta-evaluation;
9 mixed-method evaluation;
10 responsive evaluation;
11 utilization-focused evaluation.

Again, as in Chapter 3, we present these approaches systematically in accordance
with a fixed format that is briefly reiterated below. For further details, we refer the
reader to the introduction to Chapter 3. In some cases, the format may be slightly
problematic in the sense that we are dealing here with methods that have emerged
quite recently, so their various aspects and characteristics may not yet be fully
understood. As the examples will show, it is almost as if the environmental policy
field is serving as a laboratory for the testing and fine-tuning of some of these
approaches.

BOX 4.1 EXPLANATORY FRAMEWORK FOR THE METHODS IN DESIGNING EVALUATION RESEARCH

Elucidation and context

- The essence of the method:
  - What?
  - When?
  - Advantages and disadvantages?
- Historical context.
- Position in research and evaluation context.

Methodology

- Steps in the application of the method.
- Remarks.

References

- Primary and additional references.
- Examples.

4.1 ADVOCATE–ADVERSARY EVALUATION

Exemplary evaluation questions relating to advocate–adversary evaluation

- How can one evaluate policies that are highly controversial and contested in situations where 'classical' evaluation approaches would only encounter mistrust?
- How should one go about assessing a contested evaluation study in a manner that allows both opponents and proponents to have their say?

4.1.1 Elucidation and context

The essence of the method

What?

Advocate–adversary evaluation is based on a juridical metaphor. The starting point is that bias on the part of the evaluator can never be reduced to zero and that one should therefore rely on several evaluators to put forward arguments for divergent viewpoints. A public hearing is organized at which every evaluator is given an opportunity to argue a case. There is a 'judge' who formulates the final conclusion (a judgment or verdict) on the basis of evidence, testimonies, expert reports and pleadings. The purpose of this judicial approach is to ensure that the public is able to form an idea of the strengths and weaknesses of the object of evaluation.

There are two variants to the advocate–adversary evaluation method. In the first, the policy-makers are supposed to defend themselves against the accusation that they have been unable to achieve their policy objectives. The second variant, in which the values and consequences of a recently completed evaluation study are assessed, complements traditional evaluation research and is intended to enhance the formation of an opinion on that research. The second variant is, in fact, a meta-evaluation (see Section 4.8 'Meta-evaluation and meta-analysis') through debate.

When?

The judicial approach to evaluation research is not applied all that often. However, it can occasionally be very useful if:

- the object of the evaluation affects a large group of people;
- an issue is causing controversy and is drawing much public attention;
- the parties involved realize how powerful a public trial can be and accept this;
- the issue in question is more or less sharply defined;

- the 'judges' enjoy a neutral image;
- sufficient resources are available to apply the method in practice.

Advantages and disadvantages?

The application of a judicial approach in evaluation research offers various advantages:

- The method creates openness and transparency with regard to the various viewpoints on the object of evaluation. The argument pros and cons can be discussed freely in an open forum.
- The model does justice to the complexity of social reality as it takes into account not only facts, but also opinions and perceptions, values and suppositions.
- The judicial approach can reduce the political controversy surrounding the object of evaluation. The data collected and the arguments presented may be informative to a broad public.
- All relevant information with regard to the object of evaluation is collated. In situations where only one actor is allowed to have a say, relevant information may be withheld for tactical reasons.
- The method is suitable for meta-evaluation (i.e. an evaluation of an evaluation study). It may also be combined with other evaluation approaches, including such expertise and participation-oriented methods as connoisseurship and criticism (see Section 4.3), deliberative democratic evaluation (see Section 4.5) and constructivist evaluation (see Section 4.4).

Advocate–adversary evaluation also presents a number of drawbacks or risks:

- The judicial approach is problematic from a political point of view as it may involve a sharp or venomous debate. Personal rancour between the parties involved can influence the course and outcome of the process. The goal must always be to optimize policy, not to pronounce guilt or innocence.
- Advocate–adversary evaluation can degenerate into needless argument, competition and mutual accusation. Since advocate–adversary evaluation is based on a conflict model, the possibilities for reaching agreement are limited.
- The main players are not always equally skilled or knowledgeable, which can influence the final outcome. Articulate individuals are at an advantage, even if their point of view is less well underpinned. Moreover, judges are not infallible. Consequently, a balanced verdict or judgment is not guaranteed.
- It is an unspoken rule that all points of view (pros and cons) should be argued equally forcibly. Yet, a verdict may be reached on the basis of incomplete information. Moreover, the use of judicial vocabulary and legal procedures can hinder the process.

- Depending upon the design, the method can be time consuming and expensive. Certainly, it requires the deployment of many individuals: advocates, witnesses, judges, experts, etc.

Historical context

Wolf (1975) pioneered the application of this judicial approach. He tested the method on the basis of a hypothetical educational curriculum. Wolf was convinced that evaluators in education would come to rely more on personal testimonies and thus be better able to gain an understanding of the multifaceted nature of their research (Wolf, 1986, p192). Levine (1974), Owens (1973), and Popham and Carlson (1983) have also applied and further developed the method.

Research and evaluation context

The legal approach with advocacy and objection is a response to the dominance of the objectifying approach in policy evaluation. This objectifying approach entails that the evaluator tries to prevent his/her personal contribution from influencing the research findings and assessment of policy. In the judicial approach, it is assumed impossible for an evaluator not to have a personal impact. Therefore, one opts not so much for scientific justification as for public accountability on the part of the evaluators.

The judicial approach aims at teaching the actors involved and the attending public about the policy (or the policy evaluation) in question. In this sense, it ties in with other participatory approaches, such as empowerment evaluation (see Section 4.6), utilization-focused evaluation (see Section 4.11), constructivist evaluation (see Section 4.4) and responsive evaluation (see Section 4.10).

As the method involves the deployment of experts and judges, it may also be regarded as an *expertise-oriented evaluation approach*.

4.1.2 Methodology

Steps in advocate–adversary evaluation

Wolf (1975) distinguishes four stages in applying the judicial approach (see Box 4.2). Owens (1973) attributes the following characteristics to the advocate–adversary evaluation procedure:

- The procedural rules must be flexible.
- There are no strict rules for the (*ex ante*) assessment of evidence. The only requirement is that the judge(s) must determine beforehand whether the evidence is admissible or not.

- The parties may be asked before the hearing to present all relevant facts, pieces of evidence and names of witnesses/experts to the judge(s).
- A copy of the complaint must, before the public hearing takes place, be submitted to the judge(s) and the defence. The defence may plead guilty to some charges and deny others.
- Witnesses are able to speak freely and may be subjected to cross-examination.
- Experts may be summoned for a statement before or during the hearing.
- Meetings of all parties involved with the judge(s) prior to the public hearing tend to soften the debate and can be conducive to a joint striving to get to the truth of the matter on the basis of relevant facts.
- Besides the two parties involved, other stakeholders may also be allowed to participate.

BOX 4.2 THE FOUR STAGES IN APPLYING THE JUDICIAL APPROACH

1 *Issue generation:* the identification and preparation of issues that may be brought up during the public hearing.
2 *Issue selection:* the elimination of issues on which there is no debate and the selection and further refinement of issues to be argued during the public hearing. Delimitation of the object of debate is also included here.
3 *Preparation of arguments:* collection of evidence and synthesis of main ideas to be used in arguments for or against.
4 *Clarification forum (the hearing):* public presentation of the complaint or elucidation of the object of debate. The evidence is subsequently presented and witnesses/experts are called. The pleas are then held and, finally, the verdict is read aloud.

References and Examples

Primary and additional references

Kourilsky, M. (1974) 'An adversary model for educational evaluation', *Evaluation Comment*, vol 4, no 2, pp3–6

Levine, M. (1974) 'Scientific method and the adversary model', *American Psychologist*, vol 29, no 9, pp661–677

Popham, W. J. and Carlson, D. (1986) 'Deep dark deficits of the adversary evaluation model', in G. F. Madaus, M. Scriven and D. L. Stufflebeam (eds) *Evaluation Models*, Kluwer-Nijhoff, Boston, MA

Thurston, P. (1978) 'Revitalizing adversary evaluation: Deep dark deficits or muddled mistaken musings', *Educational Researcher*, vol 7, no 7, pp3–8

Owens, T. (1973) 'Education evaluation by adversary proceeding', in E. R. House (ed) *School Evaluation: The Politics and Process*, McCutchan, Berkeley, CA

Wolf, R. L. (1975) 'Trial by jury: A new evaluation method', *Phi Delta Kappan*, vol 57, no 3, pp185–187

Example

Tableman, M.A. (1990), 'San Juan national forest mediation', in J. E. Crowfoot and J. M. Wondolleck (eds) *Environmental Disputes: Community Involvement in Conflict Resolution*, Island Press, Washington, DC

The San Juan National Forest mediation case describes a site-specific dispute over logging and road-building in a scenic Colorado national forest. The process was mediated by two professional mediators and involved representatives of the US Department of Agriculture (USDA) Forest Service, local businesses, federal and state environmental organizations, and timber companies. The dispute shifted to an environmental dispute settlement after escalating in the agency administrative decision-making.

4.2 CONTEXT, INPUT, PROCESS AND PRODUCT EVALUATION: THE CIPP MODEL

Exemplary evaluation questions relating to the CIPP model

- How can one make a broad and overall evaluation of the context, the input, the processes and the products of a policy programme, rather than a topical evaluation of a specific policy measure?
- How should one go about making a policy evaluation that covers a policy (sub-) domain in general?

4.2.1 Elucidation and context

The essence of the method

What?
Stufflebeam (1966, 1967, 1972, 1993) greatly influenced the development of the so-called CIPP model. He developed a framework for policy evaluation that would assist policy-makers in four types of decision-making:

1   *Context evaluation*, in order to make decisions regarding the appropriateness of policy intentions. Before policy decisions are taken, a thorough analysis should be made of the context in which that policy is to be implemented. Policy should be geared towards existing needs.
2   *Input evaluation*, in order to structure decision-making. Determining what means are available, exploring policy alternatives and weighing up one's policy options can all help to determine the manner in which policy should be conducted.
3   *Process evaluation*, in order to underpin decisions on policy implementation. How well is a plan executed? Which bottlenecks pose a potential threat to policy success? Which policy aspects need fine-tuning? Once these questions have been answered, one may proceed with evaluating and refining the formal procedures.
4   *Product evaluation*, with a view to recycling previous decisions. Which results have been achieved? To what extent have the policy issues been resolved? What is the future of projects that have been executed? These questions are important in assessing policy achievements.

Together, the first letter of each type of evaluation – context, input, process and product – form the acronym CIPP. Table 4.1 summarizes the principal characteristics of the four evaluation types.

In more recent publications, Stufflebeam (2003) further develops the element of product evaluation. The central question of whether or not policy works is complemented by four additional questions:

1 Is the target group being reached and have they adapted their behaviour (impact)?
2 Has the policy issue been resolved (goal attainment)?
3 Are the positive policy results continuing (sustainability)?
4 Are the processes that have contributed to the success of policy readily transferable and adaptable to other contexts (transportability)?

When?

The CIPP model is an encompassing evaluation framework that applies to policy programmes, policy projects, organizations and systems. It is, however, not intended for specific sub-studies into context, input, process or products. The CIPP model ties in with the systemic approach in which policy-makers are constantly supported by evaluative information during the policy decision-making process. In this way, the CIPP model approximates the closest to an evaluation from an institutional perspective, as described in Chapter 1.

The flowchart in Figure 4.1 clarifies when (under which circumstances) specific components of the CIPP model are relevant and need to be worked out further.

Advantages and disadvantages?

The CIPP model has a number of advantages.

• The information that is collected for applying the CIPP model can be used in interpreting and explaining the policy results.
• The CIPP model, thanks to its systematic approach, also yields information that is useful in stimulating and planning policy change.
• Since the evaluation is embedded in the policy implementation, the policy relevance of the evaluation is greater.
• The application of context, input, process and product evaluation is, moreover, not recommended in a standard way. Its application depends upon the information requirements of the policy-makers (see Figure 4.1).

There has also been criticism of the approach:

• Since they provide data and make an *ex ante* evaluation of the policy options, the evaluators have an important impact upon the decision-making process. The fact that, in the CIPP approach, policy evaluation is embedded in the

Table 4.1 *Four types of evaluation in the CIPP model*

	Context evaluation	Input evaluation
Objective	Define the institutional context; identify the target population and assess their needs; identify opportunities for addressing needs; diagnose *problems* underlying the *needs*; judge whether proposed objectives are sufficiently responsive to the assessed needs	Identify and assess *system capabilities,* alternative programme *strategies,* procedural *designs* for implementing the strategies, budgets and schedules
Method	Use such methods as system analysis, survey, document review, hearings, interviews, diagnostic tests, and the Delphi technique	Inventory and analyse available human and material resources, solution strategies and procedural designs for relevance, feasibility and economy; use such methods as literature search, visits to exemplary programmes, advocacy teams and pilot trials
Relation to decision-making in the change process	Decide upon the *setting* to be served, the *goals* associated with meeting needs or using opportunities, and the *objectives* associated with solving problems (i.e. for *planning* needed changes and for providing a basis for judging outcomes)	Select *sources of support*, solution *strategies* and procedural *designs* (i.e. for *structuring* change activities and to provide a basis for judging implementation)

Source: Stufflebeam (1983, p129), reproduced with permission of the author and publisher

policy-making system is seen by some as a threat to the objectivity of the results of the evaluation study.

- The CIPP method takes a rational view of policy. In this approach, the evaluator proceeds on the assumption that policy decisions are primarily taken on the basis of evaluative data. However, this is not the case. After all, the balance of power, the organizational characteristics and the nature of the issue at hand are at least as important in decision-making.
- The combination of the four types of evaluation (context, input, process and product evaluation) is complex as the evaluators must deal with all the specific problems and limitations relevant to the different types of analysis. In order to be able to carry out the four sub-evaluations successfully, the evaluators require a great deal of (consolidated) knowledge and experience.

Process evaluation	*Product evaluation*
Identify or predict, in process, *defects* in the procedural design of its implementation; provide information for the pre-programmed decisions; record and judge procedural events and activities	Collect descriptions and judgements of outcomes and relate them to objectives; place in context, input and process information; interpret their work and merit
Monitor the activity's potential procedural barriers and remain alert to unanticipated ones; obtain specified information for programmed decisions; describe the actual process; continually interact with and observe the activities of project staff	Define operationally and measure outcome criteria; collect the judgements of outcomes from stakeholders; perform both qualitative and quantitative analyses
Implement and refine the programme design and procedure (i.e. to effect *process control* and to provide a log of the actual process for later use in interpreting outcomes)	Decide to *continue, terminate, modify or refocus* a change activity, and present a clear record of effects (intended and unintended; positive and negative)

Historical context

The CIPP model was originally developed during the late 1960s. It has since been adapted on four occasions:

1 The original version (Stufflebeam, 1966) emphasized the need to combine process and product evaluation.
2 The second version, which was published a year later (Stufflebeam, 1967), made a distinction between context, input, process and product evaluation. It was asserted that determining the policy goals went hand in hand with context evaluation (including needs analysis; see Section 3.1 in Chapter 3) and that policy planning should be coupled with input evaluation (including comparison of policy options).

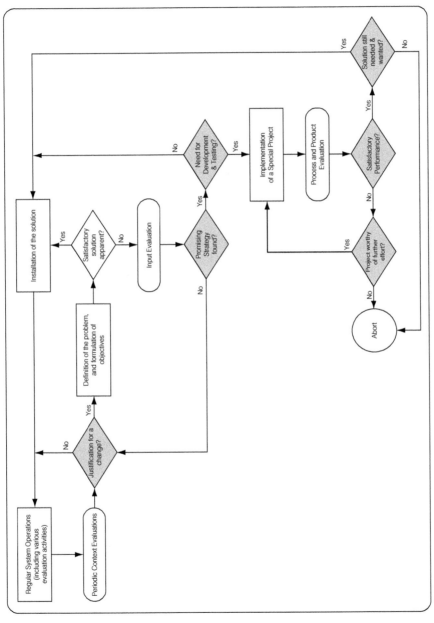

Figure 4.1 *Flowchart for applying the CIPP model*

Source: Stufflebeam (1986, p126), reproduced with permission of the author and publisher; shading added by Crabbé and Leroy

3   The third version of the CIPP model (Stufflebeam et al, 1971) places the four evaluative components (context, input, process and product) in a framework for policy enhancement.
4   In the fourth version (Stufflebeam, 1972), it is argued that the CIPP model can, and must be, used for 'learning about policy'.
5   Version five divides product evaluation into four components with a view to a longer-term evaluation of policy progress.

The model was used and further refined by Adams (1971), Root (1971), Reinhard (1972), Nevo (1974), Webster (1975) and Findlay (1979), among others.

Research and evaluation context

The CIPP model ties in with the *management-oriented approaches* to evaluation research. These approaches aim specifically at assisting policy-makers in reaching policy decisions. By distinguishing between various types of policy decisions, the management-oriented approaches specify who will apply the evaluation results, how they should use them and about which aspects of the system the policy-maker is required to make choices. The information needs of the policy-maker are decisive in the design and execution of the evaluation study.

4.2.2 Methodology

Steps in CIPP evaluation

Stufflebeam (1986, p138) provides the following outline of steps to be undertaken when preparing for a CIPP evaluation:

1   review of the charge;
2   plan for obtaining information;
3   plan for reporting the results;
4   plan for administering the study.

Review of the charge
This step comprises the following:

•   definition of the object of the evaluation;
•   identification of the client and audiences;
•   purpose(s) of the evaluation;
•   type of evaluation (e.g. context, input, process or product) to be employed;
•   principles of sound evaluation (i.e. standards) to be observed.

Plan for obtaining information

The plan includes the following:

- the general strategy;
- working assumptions to guide measurement, analysis and interpretation;
- collection of information (i.e. sampling, instrumentation and data collection);
- organization of information (i.e. coding, filing and retrieving);
- analysis of information (both qualitative and quantitative);
- interpretation of findings.

Plan for reporting the results

This plan features:

- preparation of reports;
- dissemination of reports;
- provision of follow-up activities to promote impact of the evaluation.

Plan for administering the study

Here, the following components are highlighted:

- summarization of the evaluation schedule;
- plan for meeting staff and resource requirements;
- provision for meta-evaluation;
- provision for periodic updating of the evaluation design;
- budget;
- memorandum of agreement or contract.

Stufflebeam also drew up a checklist of items to look out for when applying the CIPP model. The table can be found at www.wmich.edu/evalctr/checklists/cipp checklist.htm, accessed 1 March 2008.

References and Examples

Primary and additional references

Adams, J. A. (1971) *A Study of the Status, Scope, and Nature of Educational Evaluation in Michigan's Public K-12 School Districts*, PhD thesis, Ohio State University at Columbus, OH

Candoli, C., Cullen, K. and Stufflebeam, D. L. (1997) 'An emerging model for superintendent evaluation', in C. Candoli, K. Cullen and D. L. Stufflebeam (eds) *Superintendent Performance Evaluation: Current Practice and Directions for Improvement*, Kluwer Academic Publishers, Boston, MA

Findlay, D. (1979) *Working Paper for Planning and Evaluation System*, Unpublished working paper, Ohio State University, Columbus, OH

Nevo, D. (1974) *Evaluation Priorities of Students, Teachers, and Principals*, PhD thesis, Ohio State University at Columbus, OH

Reinhard, D. L. (1972) *Methodology Development for Input Evaluation Using Advocate and Design Teams*, PhD thesis, Ohio State University at Columbus, OH

Root, D. (1971) *The Evaluation Training Needs of Superintendents of Schools*, PhD thesis, Ohio State University at Columbus, OH

Stufflebeam, D. L. (1966) 'A depth study of the evaluation requirement', *Theory into Practice*, vol 5, no 3, pp121–133

Stufflebeam, D. L. (1967) 'The use and abuse of evaluation in title III', *Theory into Practice*, vol 6, no 3, pp126–133

Stufflebeam, D. L. (1972) 'The relevance of the CIPP evaluation model for educational accountability', *SRIS Quarterly*, vol 5, no 1, pp19–25

Stufflebeam, D. L. (1983) 'The CIPP model for program evaluation', in G. F. Madaus, M. Scriven and D. L. Stufflebeam (eds) *Evaluation Models*, Kluwer-Nijhoff, Boston, MA

Stufflebeam, D. L. (1986) 'The CIPP model for program evaluation', in G. F. Madaus, M. Scriven and D. L. Stufflebeam (eds) *Evaluation Models: Viewpoints on Educational and Human Services Evaluation*, Kluwer-Nijhoff, Boston, MA

Stufflebeam, D. L. (2003) 'The CIPP model for evaluation', in D. L. Stufflebeam and T. Kellaghan (eds) *The international handbook of educational evaluation*, Kluwer Academic Publishers, Boston, MA

Stufflebeam, D. L. (2004) 'The 21st-century CIPP model: Origins, development and use', in M. C. Alkin (ed) *Evaluation Roots: Tracing Theorists' Views and Influences*, Sage, London

Stufflebeam, D. L., Foley, W. J., Gephart, W. J., Hammond, L. R., Merriman, H. O. and Provus, M. M. (1971) *Educational Evaluation and Decision Making*, F. E. Peacock, Itasca, IL

Webster, W. J. (1975) 'The organization and functions of research and evaluation in large urban school districts', paper presented at the annual meeting of the American Educational Research Association, Washington, DC

Examples

The CIPP approach has been applied to many policy programme contexts, especially in education policy in the US. Examples of applications in education can be found in the doctoral theses by Adams (1971), Nevo (1974) and Root (1971).

Andrew, J. S. (2001) 'Examining the claims of environmental ADR: Evidence from waste management conflicts in Ontario and Massachusetts', *Journal of Planning Education and Research*, vol 21, no 2, pp166–183

The literature has established many claims concerning the effectiveness of alternative dispute resolution (ADR) in resolving environmental conflicts, with little empirical research to support them. Using data collected from 54 recent cases in which ADR was used to resolve waste management disputes in Ontario and Massachusetts, this study employs seven criteria of success to test empirically the effectiveness of alternative dispute resolution in resolving environmental conflicts.

4.3 CONNOISSEURSHIP AND CRITICISM

Exemplary evaluation questions relating to connoisseurship and criticism

- How do (one or several) eminent external expert(s) assess a particular societal issue and the way in which policy-makers try to respond to it?
- How do experts, well involved and yet with distance, judge a certain policy?

4.3.1 Elucidation and context

The essence of the method

What?

The key concept behind the approach is that certain experts possess the ability to give clear, relevant and inspiring accounts of the quality and significance of policy (practices) on the basis of their personal knowledge and skills. Much like critics are asked to pronounce their opinions in the world of art and culture, so experts are requested to form judgements on practices within their field of expertise. Their assignment is to describe and assess policy (practices) and to elucidate their merits and shortcomings.

The connoisseurship and criticism approach does not fit into the dominant scientific paradigm; but, then, that was never the intention of those who developed it. They see connoisseurship and criticism as an artistic activity that provides a qualitative, subjective and, thus, non-orthodox scientific complement to the traditional objectifying evaluation methods. In their view, the traditional approaches are found lacking in that they ignore the positivist bias which they introduce into the evaluation process. Moreover, they tend to reproduce and confirm existing policy views without much criticism.

Connoisseurship is the art of appraisal, not in the sense of appreciation or preference, but in the sense of an awareness of an object's characteristics. The connoisseur is aware of the complexity of reality and possesses an excellent capacity for observation that allows him or her to gauge and assess that complexity. Their exceptional capacity for observation consists in knowing what to look for, a skill which the connoisseur has developed through a backlog of relevant experience (Worthen, 1997, p128). Connoisseurs in policy evaluation are comparable to wine experts who are able to describe and judge the essential characteristics of a vintage. However, connoisseurship does not require a public rendering of what the experts observe, as this would come close to the realm of criticism.

'Criticism is the art of disclosing the qualities of events or objects that connoisseurship perceives' (Eisner, in Worthen, 1997, p129). In this context, criticism is not necessarily a negative appraisal. It is, rather, an educational message in which the expert clarifies what are the essential characteristics of the evaluation object, which otherwise might well have remained unnoticed. The assignment of the critic is to explain the positive and negative characteristics of the evaluation object in a clear and expressive manner in order to generate a dynamic. He or she may draw parallels with other situations and will select a wording that is intended to open up eyes. Qualitative criticism requires connoisseurship; but connoisseurship does not necessarily imply criticism: 'connoisseurship is private ... criticism is public' (Eisner, 1986, p340).

When?
This approach is appropriate in specific circumstances where:

- the evaluation also involves a non-scientific (i.e. ethical and political) appraisal;
- policy-makers (politicians and civil servants) are trying to get issues on the political and social agenda at the suggestion of others;
- a policy issue is causing controversy and a public trial approach (see Section 4.1 'Advocate–adversary evaluation') is politically or socially too sensitive;
- the time or means are lacking to apply other, more participatory, evaluation methods, such as empowerment evaluation (see Section 4.6), responsive evaluation (see Section 4.10), deliberative democratic evaluation (see Section 4.5), utilization-focused evaluation (see Section 4.11) or constructivist evaluation (see Section 4.4).
- experts are found willing and able to make their knowledge and expertise available.

Advantages and disadvantages?
The main advantage of the approach is that it allows one to rely on specific knowledge and gradually acquired insights of individuals who have devoted much time and energy to studying the topic in question. Experts can contribute a whole range of relevant information that the general public may subsequently rely on to arrive at a complementary and more detailed assessment than might otherwise have been the case.

The disadvantage of the approach is that the results are entirely dependent upon the capabilities of the expert who gives his/her appraisal, where there is a realistic chance that biased and subjective views are transferred. The approach stands or falls with the knowledge and skills of the expert in question. It is, moreover, crucially important that the target group should trust the expert and be willing to accept his/her evaluative conclusions as truthful.

Historical context

Connoisseurship and criticism is a less well-known evaluation method that is applied in education evaluation by a research group at Stanford University, US. Eisner is the driving force and inspiration behind the approach. About a dozen members of his group have conducted research using this method, contributing to the further development of the connoisseurship and criticism approach. These other exponents include Greer (1973), Vallance (1974) and Flinders and Eisner (2000).

Research and evaluation context

Connoisseurship and criticism relies entirely on the use of subjective professional expertise as a strategy for evaluation policy programmes. For this reason, the method belongs to the *expertise-oriented evaluation approaches*.

4.3.2 Methodology

Steps in connoisseurship and criticism

According to Eisner (1986), connoisseurship is the art of appreciation, while criticism is the art of disclosure. Criticism consists of three central components (Eisner, 1986, p341), as outlined in Box 4.3.

BOX 4.3 THE THREE CENTRAL COMPONENTS OF CRITICISM

1 Description of the policy programme and its context, with emphasis on the most relevant characteristics.
2 Interpretation of what has been described in order to explain meaning and significance.
3 Evaluation of the policy programme in order to arrive at an assessment of the described and interpreted data.

References and Examples

Primary and additional references

Eisner, E. W. (1975) 'The perceptive eye: Toward the reformation of educational evaluation', Unpublished invited address at the American Educational Research Association, Washington, DC
Eisner, E. W. (1979a) *The Educational Imagination: On the Design and Evaluation of School Programs*, Macmillan, New York, NY
Eisner, E. W. (1979b) 'The use of qualitative forms of evaluation for improving educational practice', *Educational Evaluation and Policy Analysis*, vol 1, no 6, pp11–19

Eisner, E. W. (1986) 'Educational connoisseurship and criticism: Their form and functions in educational evaluation', in G. F. Madaus, M. Scriven and D. L. Stufflebeam (eds) *Evaluation Models: Viewpoints on Educational and Human Services Evaluation*, Kluwer-Nijhoff, Boston, MA

Eisner, E. W. (1991) 'Taking a second look: Educational connoisseurship revisited', in M. W. McLaughlin and D. C. Phillips (eds) *Evaluation and Education: A Quarter Century. Yearbook of the National Society for the Study of Education, Part II*, University of Chicago Press, Chicago, IL

Eisner, E. W. (1998) *The Enlightened Eye: Qualitative inquiry and the Enhancement of Educational Practice*, Prentice Hall, Upper Saddle River, NY

Flinders, D. J. and Eisner, E. W. (2000) 'Educational criticism as a form of qualitative inquiry', in D. L. Stufflebeam, G. F. Madaus and T. Kellaghan (eds) *Evaluation Models*, Kluwer, Boston, MA

Greer, D. (1973) *The Criticism of Teaching*, PhD thesis, Stanford University at Palo Alto, CA

Vallence, E. (1974) *Aesthetic Criticism and Curriculum Description*, PhD thesis, Stanford University at Palo Alto, CA

Worthen, B. R., Sanders, J. R. and Fitzpatrick, J. L. (1997) *Program Evaluation: Alternative Approaches and Practical Guidelines*, 2nd edition, Longman Publishers, New York, NY

Examples

In France, 'committees of wise men' have been set up either temporarily (e.g. the French Nationality Commission during 1986 to 1987) or have become standing committees, as is the case with the French National Ethics Committee (*Comité National d'Éthique*), set up in 1983, and the High Council for Integration (*Haut Conseil à l'Intégration*), established in 1989.

Also, in a broader European context, the idea of 'committees of wise men' is not exceptional. In 2007, French President Sarkozy suggested, for example, creating a committee of wise men to consider the European Union's future: up to 12 'highly respected personalities' would be mandated to produce a plan for the development of the EU until the year 2030.

4.4 CONSTRUCTIVIST EVALUATION

Exemplary evaluation questions relating to constructivist evaluation

- How might one evaluate in order to encourage policy-makers to reflect upon their own frames of reference, problem definitions and other assumptions when undertaking policy action?
- How can one elucidate and evaluate the assumptions and logics underlying certain policies?

4.4.1 Elucidation and context

Although Guba and Lincoln (1985) initially referred to their approach as naturalistic enquiry, it is now known as constructivist evaluation. This change of name, however, did not coincide with essential changes in terms of content and approach.

The essence of the method

What?

As an approach, constructivist evaluation is philosophically inspired. It is based on the constructivist paradigm and fits within a participatory approach.

Philosophically inspired. The constructivist method is opposed to the rational-positivist approach to conducting an evaluation study. Lincoln and Guba, the founders of constructivist evaluation, assert that there are no absolute answers to evaluation questions. They oppose the dominant notion that human bias needs to be eliminated from evaluation research and argue for the recognition of the role of diverse values in (policy) evaluation.

In constructivist evaluation, much attention is paid to the description and elucidation of policy contexts in a participatory process involving stakeholders in the policy process. The central purpose is to acquire insight into the perception (or 'constructions') that stakeholders have vis-à-vis policy and policy-making. While one construction is no more accurate than another, some are considered to be superior because they are based on more extensive information and have been developed in a more sophisticated way. The evaluative conclusions that are drawn in constructivist evaluation are never definitive: the possibility that other, possibly better, answers may be formulated is always left open. The evaluative conclusions reached are, moreover, not universally valid: they are context dependent.

Constructivist paradigm. Constructivist evaluation is closely linked with the constructivist paradigm. This paradigm is based on three fundamental assumptions: an ontological, an epistemological and a methodological assumption:

1   The basic ontological assumption of constructivism is *relativism*. The key
     notion here is that all knowledge is comparative. Individuals construct reality
     by attributing meaning to their experiences. There is no objective reality that
     underpins their views.
2   The basic epistemological assumption of constructivism is *transactional
     subjectivism*. Assertions about reality depend solely upon the information and
     degree of sophistication available to the individuals and upon their mutual
     interaction.
3   The basic methodological assumption behind constructivism is *hermeneutic
     dialecticism*, a process where constructions entertained by different
     individuals are first inventoried and analysed, and subsequently confronted,
     compared and contrasted. The first of these (sub-) processes is hermeneutic;
     the second is dialectic.

Participation. The approach attributes a central role to the evaluators and
stakeholders in the research. The evaluators may (must, even) organize the evaluation
in such a way that the stakeholders are emancipated, and are able to acquire
knowledge and insight in order to protect their interests. The evaluators should
encourage the stakeholders to increase their awareness of the (policy) situation. They
are stimulated, informed and supported in their effort to change and improve an
unsatisfactory situation. For emancipatory reasons, the stakeholders are attributed a
central role in determining the evaluation questions: they must, in consultation,
decide which evaluation topics are more important than others.

When?
Constructivist evaluation is useful in situations where the key policy players have
opposing opinions that stand in the way of smooth cooperation. The approach is
only meaningful in cases where those key players are prepared to have their
opinions critically assessed.

Advantages and disadvantages?
Guba and Lincoln recognize the following strengths in their approach (Madaus
et al, 1986, p313):

*   *'It offers a contextual relevance and richness that is unmatched.'* From a
    constructivist point of view, a policy can only be understood fully if it is
    considered in its natural environment. For this reason, the evaluator must be
    open to the context in which policy is conducted and must try to understand
    how policy is experienced by policy-makers, implementers and stakeholders.
*   *'It displays a sensitivity to process virtually excluded in paradigms stressing control and
    experimentation.'* Constructivist evaluation adopts a very open attitude towards
    the evaluation process and outcomes. The approach insists on involving all

stakeholders who may benefit from or be damaged by the evaluation. They are involved with a view to enhancing their positions within the policy process. After all, constructivist evaluation also has an emancipatory function.

- *'It is driven by theory grounded in the data – the naturalist does not search for data that fit a theory but develops a theory to explain the data.'* This is in stark contrast to the orthodox scientific paradigm according to which a theory drives the data collection process. The notion of a theory that is underpinned by data about reality was launched by Glaser and Strauss (1967) and was subsequently adopted by naturalistic constructivist researchers because they found that the unstructured complexity of reality made it virtually impossible to develop an *a priori* theory.

- *'Naturalistic approaches take full advantage of the not inconsiderable power of the human as instrument, providing a more than adequate trade-off for the presumably more objective approach that characterises rationalistic enquiry.'* In constructivist evaluation, the evaluators and stakeholders occupy a central position in the research process, where they are used as 'human tools' in the evaluation. Their experiences, knowledge and values are deployed in the evaluation project so that no technical means for data collection need be developed and tested, nor do the data need to be validated.

Constructivist evaluation has a number of relevant disadvantages. The first set of weaknesses concerns the fact that the constructivist approach hinges on the participation of a broad group of stakeholders (Stufflebeam, 2001, p74):

- Given the need for involving many individuals and the possibility of constant interaction, it is difficult to report in a timely fashion to the client who has requested the evaluation.
- Not all policy stakeholders will be prepared to participate in a constructivist evaluation. Moreover, it is not easy to find people whose outlook on policy is sufficiently broad and who are adequately informed about the technical and practical aspects of policy-making. It is unrealistic to expect evaluators to invest time in informing and training people in order to take part in the evaluation.
- The evaluation process can, moreover, be hindered by the degree of mobility within the stakeholder group: people come and go so that closed discussions are sometimes reopened and previously drawn conclusions are called into question again.
- While much attention is paid in constructivist evaluation to openness and clarity, participants in the evaluation process are not always prepared to share their ideas and personal analyses.

Moreover, a further weakness of the approach is that clients and participants may not be happy with the fact that the evaluators are prepared to highlight contradictory, sometimes diametrically opposed, opinions on policy-making, while at the same time refraining from adopting a position on the merits and shortcomings of policy. Many people are unaccustomed to the constructivist philosophy and prefer reports that provide so-called hard data and statistically significant assessments on policy outcomes (Stufflebeam, 2001, p74).

Historical context

Guba and Lincoln pioneered the constructivist approach. Bhola (1998), a pupil of Guba's, applied the approach to evaluate policy projects in Africa. He asserts that evaluation research is affected not only by the method applied and the degree of interaction with the stakeholders, but also by the personal experiences and opinions of the evaluator. Schwandt (1984), another disciple of Guba's, has written extensively on the philosophical foundations of the constructivist approach.

Research and evaluation context

Constructivist evaluation – like empowerment evaluation, responsive evaluation, utilisation-focused evaluation and deliberative democratic evaluation – attaches great importance to the participation of the various stakeholders. These participatory or interactive approaches to policy evaluation involve knowledge input by practical and experiential experts because such knowledge can be very useful in gaining a better understanding of policy practice and in formulating relevant and practicable policy recommendations.

Constructivist evaluation does differ from the other participatory methods in a number of ways:

- Constructivist evaluation differs from *empowerment evaluation* in terms of the role that is attributed to the evaluator. While in the constructivist approach, the evaluator retains control of the evaluation process and cooperates with the stakeholders in trying to attain consensus, in empowerment evaluation, the evaluator relinquishes part of his power to the stakeholders and restricts his or her contribution to a supporting role.
- The difference with *responsive evaluation* lies in who takes responsibility for the research design. While in responsive evaluation, the research design is shaped, in part, by the stakeholders, in the case of constructivist evaluation, responsibility for the research design lies entirely with the evaluator.
- *Utilization-focused evaluation*, like constructivist evaluation, aims at enhancing the practical value of the evaluation results; but utilization-focused evaluation does not put forward a specific evaluation model, method or technique, while constructivist evaluation clearly does (compare with the notion of 'constructions').

- *Deliberative democratic evaluation* (DDE) differs from constructivist evaluation in the sense that DDE, more so than constructivist evaluation, is suitable for application in conflict situations. Without a 'detour' via constructions, DDE strives towards participation on the part of all stakeholders, open debate and the drawing of conclusions.

4.4.2 Methodology

Steps in constructivist evaluation

Constructivist evaluation is applied in steps. Although in Box 4.4 this is represented as a sequential process, it is possible, in practice, that certain steps are blocked, that the process has to start anew, that steps are skipped, etc. The sequential representation of the steps is merely for didactic reasons. Let us

---

BOX 4.4 THE ELEVEN STEPS
IN CONSTRUCTIVIST EVALUATION

Step 1: Organize the evaluation.
↓
Step 2: Identify and involve the stakeholders.
↓
Step 3: Inventory, analyse and compare the constructions entertained by the group members.
↓
Step 4: Test the constructions of the evaluator against other constructions.
↓
Step 5: Order topics on which the group members are in agreement.
↓
Step 6: Order topics on which the group members have not reached consensus.
↓
Step 7: Collect additional information and refine existing knowledge.
↓
Step 8: Prepare an agenda for negotiation by selecting and clearly formulating rival opinions.
↓
Step 9: Inventory, analyse and compare constructions of non-group members.
↓
Step 10: Report on results of step 9.
↓
Step 11: Reiterate the process for those topics that could not be resolved in step 9.

begin our description of the steps at the stage where evaluators and clients have already made contractual agreements about the execution of a constructivist evaluation.

Organizing the evaluation

This entails composing the core group of (professional) evaluators drawing up a plan of action, making logistical preparations and assessing political and cultural factors that may influence the outcome.

Identifying and involving the stakeholders

This implies ascertaining who the policy-makers and policy implementers are, as well as determining the composition of the policy target group. The evaluation identifies target group members who stand to benefit from policy, as well as 'victims'. Subsequently, a representative delegation is formally requested to participate in the evaluation process.

Inventorying, analysing and comparing the constructions that the group members entertain

Groups of 10 to 12 individuals are formed, each of which represents a group who is involved in the policy programme. In these groups, policy is described (i.e. joint 'constructions' are made), the various interests are declared, bottlenecks are indicated and positive (side) effects are specified. The purpose of group conversations is to reach consensus within the group on as many topics as possible.

Testing the constructions of the evaluators against other constructions

The groups of stakeholders are confronted with other 'constructions' of reality. Their perceptions are tested against those of the evaluators, the available documentation about the object of evaluation, the data collected by the evaluators (in interviews, through participatory observation or by means of documents analysis) and other sources that are deemed relevant.

Ordering topics on which the group members agree

If there is agreement on certain issues discussed within the group, then these are set aside so that they can be picked up again at a later stage when the research report is being compiled.

Ordering topics on which the group members do not agree

If group members have opposing views on certain issues, then these are selected for subsequent debate. The order in which these topics will be discussed later should be determined in consultation by the group members.

Collecting additional information and refining existing knowledge

In order to try and reach consensus on topics on which there was initially no agreement, ways are sought to help the negotiation process forward. The evaluators assess their own operational strategy, additional information is possibly gathered, and/or the available data are reinterpreted and/or presented in a different way.

Preparing an agenda for negotiation by selecting and elucidating rival opinions

In step 8, practical preparations are made for fresh negotiations on topics that could previously not be resolved. This requires a new plan of approach: the preparation of (newly) obtained data for presentation, etc. (see step 7: collecting additional information and refining existing knowledge).

Inventorying, analysing and comparing constructions entertained by non-group members

In step 9, steps 3 to 8 are reiterated for a newly composed group. This group consists of individuals selected by the previous group members as their substitutes/representatives. The outcome of step 9 is a set of broadly supported conceptions of the policy object, its shortcomings and merits. Those topics on which the group members are unable to reach consensus are set aside in order to be recycled during a subsequent negotiation cycle (see step 11: reiterating the process for those topics that could not be resolved in step 9).

Reporting on the results of step 9

It is not unthinkable that several research reports are written in the evaluation process: (sub-) reports that take into account the specific needs of the stakeholders involved. If there is consensus within the group on policy recommendations, then obviously these may be described in a general report on the evaluation process.

Reiterating the process for those topics that could not be resolved in step 9

This recycling of topics demonstrates that constructivist evaluation is a cyclical process.

References and Examples

Primary and additional references

Bhola, H. S. (1998) 'Program evaluation for program renewal: A study of the national literacy program in Namibia (NLPN)', *Studies in Educational Evaluation*, vol 24, no 4, pp303–330

Erlandson, D. A., Harris, E. L., Skipper, B. L. and Allen, S. D. (1993) *Doing Naturalistic Inquiry: A Guide to Methods*, Sage, London

Glaser, B. G. and Strauss, A. L. (1967) *The Discovery of Grounded Theory: Strategies for Qualitative Research*, Aldine, Chicago, IL

Guba, E. G. and Lincoln, Y. S. (1986) 'Epistemological and methodological bases of naturalistic inquiry', in G. F. Madaus, M. Scriven and D. L. Stufflebeam (eds) *Evaluation Models: Viewpoints on Educational and Human Services Evaluation*, Kluwer-Nijhoff, Boston, MA

Guba, E. G. and Lincoln, Y. S. (1989) *Fourth Generation Evaluation*, Sage, Newbury Park, CA

Lincoln, Y. S. and Guba, E. G. (1985) *Naturalistic Inquiry*, Sage, Beverly Hills, CA

Schwandt, T. A. (1984) *An Examination of Alternative Models for Sociobehavioral Inquiry*, PhD thesis, Indiana University at Bloomington, IN

Stufflebeam, D. L. (2001) 'Evaluation models', *New Directions for Evaluation*, no 89

Examples

Elshout-Mohr, M., Oostdam, R. and Overmaat, M. (2002) 'Student assessment within the context of constructivist educational settings', *Studies in Educational Evaluation*, vol 28, no 4, pp369–390

Constructivist evaluation is commonly applied in the evaluation of educational policy programmes. Researchers with the University of Amsterdam applied the constructivist approach in an evaluation of the educational needs of youngsters in vocational training. The main findings were that a high degree of individualization was reached; but respondents had serious concerns about the lack of standardization of the assessment criteria and about the meagre check on students' available expert knowledge.

Lay, M. and Papadopoulos, I. (2007) 'An exploration of fourth generation evaluation in practice', *Evaluation*, vol 13, no 4, pp495–504

In this article the applicability of fourth-generation evaluation is explored in relation to an evaluation of a Sure Start project undertaken by the authors in 2004. Sure Start is a central government initiative established in 1999 to help fight child poverty and social exclusion in England. The authors conclude that constructivist principles provided an excellent opportunity for the different stakeholder groups to reflect on the project and deepen their knowledge and understanding of one another's perspectives and values.

4.5 DELIBERATIVE DEMOCRATIC EVALUATION

Exemplary evaluation questions relating to deliberative democratic evaluation

- How can one engage in policy evaluation in cases of conflictual relationships between the stakeholders involved when whatever outcome would encounter mistrust and provoke new conflicts?
- How can one, instead of sharpening the conflict, engage in conflict mediation through evaluation?

4.5.1 Elucidation and context

The essence of the method

What?

Deliberative democratic evaluation is one of the most recently developed approaches to evaluation research. The approach obliges evaluators to apply democratic principles when drawing evaluative conclusions on policy. The aspiration is to reach carefully considered conclusions in relation to issues on which opinions differ. In many ways, deliberative democratic evaluation resembles a Socratic dialogue on policy.

House and Howe (1998b, p93), the founders of the approach, define deliberative democratic evaluation as follows:

> *Include conflicting values and stakeholder groups in the study. Make sure all major views are sufficiently included and represented. Bring conflicting views together so there can be deliberation and dialogue about them among the relevant parties. Not only make sure there is sufficient room for dialogue to resolve conflicting claims, but help the policy-makers and media resolve these claims by sorting through the good and bad information. Bring the interests of beneficiaries to the table if they are neglected.*

Three guiding principles are central to the application of deliberative democratic evaluation – inclusion (or participation), dialogue and deliberation:

1   *Participation*: the evaluation study should consider the interests, values and views of the major stakeholders involved in the policy under review. This does not mean that every interest, value or view should be attributed equal weight, only that all relevant ones should be considered. The evaluator must prevent

certain stakeholders from having a dominant influence on the conclusions drawn through the evaluation.

2   *Dialogue*: the evaluation study should encourage extensive dialogue with stakeholder groups and, occasionally, dialogue among stakeholders. The purpose is to prevent misunderstanding of interests, values and views. However, the evaluator is under no obligation to accept views at face value. Nor should understanding be confused with agreement. The evaluator is responsible for organizing and structuring the dialogue.

3   *Deliberation*: the evaluation study should provide for mediation between actors with divergent opinions. The evaluator goes through all of the relevant issues with the participants. The evaluator remains responsible, however, for formulating conclusions in the evaluation report on the merits and shortcomings of the policy under consideration. To this end, he or she carefully weighs up arguments for and against.

In deliberative democratic evaluation, participation, dialogue and deliberation are considered to be relevant in every step of the evaluation process: as the evaluation assignment is awarded; in the research design phase; in its execution; in the analysis of results; during synthesis of the conclusions; in reporting; in the presentation of findings; and in the ensuing debate on the added value of the evaluation study.

When?
Deliberative democratic evaluation is useful in situations where there are (not excessively polarized) conflicts regarding the goals of policy or the resources to be deployed for policy-making. The method is also suitable for reconciling claims to space: an area-specific issue with which spatial planning or environmental agencies or institutions are commonly confronted.

Advantages and disadvantages?
Deliberative democratic evaluation offers at least three advantages:

1   The main merit is that the evaluator and the client consciously strive to draw correct and equitable conclusions.
2   Because of the participatory approach, the participants in the evaluation process are, moreover, encouraged to respect and use the evaluation conclusions, which enhance the policy relevancy of the study.
3   A third advantage is that the evaluator retains the right to consider the contribution of certain stakeholders as incorrect or unethical. The evaluator is open to all opinions and weighs them up carefully. Ultimately, though, it is he or she (rather than the stakeholders involved in the evaluation) who draws the conclusions.

There are also some drawbacks:

- The evaluation approach can be difficult or even impossible to apply in practice. From the moment that there is a power imbalance between the actors, and one or several of the actors decide to veto a decision, the evaluation process is in danger of grinding to a standstill. This is a latent but real threat to any deliberative democratic evaluation process.
- The expertise and neutrality of the evaluator must be recognized explicitly by all of the stakeholders. Any doubt about the evaluator may be seen as a reason by the stakeholders not to participate in deliberation or to call into question the evaluation outcome.

Historical context

House is the pioneer of this approach. He and Howe believe that many evaluators actually apply the guiding principles of deliberative democratic evaluation and that therefore the approach is not new in terms of its content. What they do regard as new and as an added value is that the main principles of democratic decision-making in evaluation research are united in a single evaluation approach.

Research and evaluation context

Deliberative democratic evaluation – like empowerment evaluation, responsive evaluation, utilization-focused evaluation and constructivist evaluation – attaches great importance to the participation of the various stakeholders. These participatory or interactive approaches to policy evaluation involve knowledge input by practical and experiential experts because such knowledge can be very useful in gaining a better understanding of policy practice and in formulating relevant and practicable policy recommendations.

Deliberative democratic evaluation does, however, differ from the other abovementioned participatory methods in a number of ways:

- *Deliberative democratic evaluation* differs from *empowerment evaluation* in terms of the role that is attributed to the evaluator. While in the deliberative democratic evaluation approach, the evaluator retains control of the evaluation process and cooperates with the stakeholders in trying to attain consensus, in empowerment evaluation, the evaluator relinquishes part of his power to the stakeholders and restricts his or her contribution to a supporting role.
- The difference from *responsive evaluation* lies in who takes responsibility for the research design. While in responsive evaluation, the research design is shaped, in part, by the stakeholders, in the case of deliberative democratic evaluation, responsibility for the research design lies entirely with the evaluator.

- *Utilization-focused evaluation*, like deliberative democratic evaluation, aims at the policy relevance of the evaluation results, although this focus is comparatively stronger in utilization-focused evaluation.
- *Constructivist evaluation* differs from deliberative democratic evaluation (DDE) in the sense that constructivist evaluation is directed more at creating clarity with regard to the underlying assumptions of policy-making.

4.5.2 Methodology

Steps in deliberative democratic evaluation

House and Howe do not propose a step-by-step approach to DDE; but they have drawn and a checklist containing 11 questions that are important when conducting this type of evaluation (House and Howe, 2000c). These questions are arranged on the basis of the three guiding principles of the approach: participation, dialogue and deliberation.

Participation

1 *Whose interests are represented in the evaluation?*
   - Specify the interests involved in the policy programme and evaluation.
   - Identify relevant interests from the history of the programme.
   - Consider important interests that emerge from the cultural context.
2 *Are all major stakeholders represented?*
   - Identify those interests not represented.
   - Seek ways of representing missing views.
   - Look for hidden commitments.
3 *Should some stakeholders be excluded?*
   - Review the reasons for excluding some stakeholders.
   - Consider if representatives represent their groups accurately.
   - Clarify the evaluator's role in organizing and structuring the evaluation.

Dialogue

4 *Do power imbalances distort or impede dialogue and deliberation?*
   - Examine the situation from the participants' point of view.
   - Consider whether participants will be forthcoming under the circumstances.
   - Consider whether some will exercise too much influence.
5 *Are there procedures to control imbalances?*
   - Do not take sides with factions.
   - Partition vociferous factions, if necessary.
   - Balance excessive self-interests.

6 *In what ways do stakeholders participate?*
- Secure commitments to rules and procedures in advance.
- Structure the exchanges carefully around specific issues.
- Structure forums in relation to participant characteristics.

7 *How authentic is the participation?*
- Do not just organize symbolic interactions.
- Address all concerns.
- Secure the views of all stakeholders.

8 *How involved is the interaction?*
- Balance depth with breadth in participation.
- Encourage receptivity to other views.
- Insist on civil discourse.

Deliberation

9 *Is there reflective deliberation?*
- Organize resources for deliberation.
- Clarify the roles of participants.
- Have experts play critical roles where relevant.

10 *How extensive is the deliberation?*
- Review the main criteria.
- Account for all the information.
- Introduce important issues neglected by stakeholders.

11 *How well considered is the deliberation?*
- Fit all the data together coherently.
- Consider likely possibilities and select the best.
- Draw the best conclusions for this context.

References and Examples

Primary and additional references

House, E. R. and Howe, K. R. (1998a) *Deliberative Democratic Evaluation in Practice*, University of Colorado, Boulder, CO

House, E. R. and Howe, K. R. (1998b) 'The issue of advocacy in evaluations', *American Journal of Evaluation*, vol 19, no 2, pp 233–236

House, E. R. and Howe, K. R. (2000a) 'Deliberative democratic evaluation', *New Directions for Evaluation*, no 85, pp3–12

House, E. R. and Howe, K. R. (2000b) 'Deliberative democratic evaluation in practice', in D. L. Stufflebeam, G. F. Madaus and T. Kellaghan (eds) *Evaluation Models*, Kluwer, Boston, MA

House, E. R. and Howe, K. R. (2000c) 'Deliberative democratic evaluation checklist', www.wmich.edu/evalctr/checklists/dd_checklist.htm, accessed 1 March 2008

Karlsson, O. (1998) 'Socratic dialogue in the Swedish political context', *New Directions for Evaluation*, no 77, pp21–38

Ryan, K. E. and DeStefano, L. (2000) 'Evaluation as a democratic process: Promoting inclusion, dialogue, and deliberation', *New Directions for Evaluation*, no 85

Examples

Lehtonen, M. (2006) 'Deliberative democracy, participation, and OECD peer reviews of environmental policies', *American Journal of Evaluation*, vol 27, no 2, pp185–200

Deliberative democracy has attracted increasing attention in political science and has been suggested as a normative ideal for evaluation. This article analyses to what extent evaluations carried out in a highly government-driven manner can, nevertheless, contribute to deliberative democracy. This potential is examined by taking the Organisation for Economic Co-operation and Development's (OECD's) environmental performance reviews as an example of an expert-led evaluative process. The author argues that although they are not participatory, these reviews lay the groundwork for deliberative democracy. This example suggests that to enhance deliberative democracy, the evaluation process need not be highly inclusive, dialogical and deliberative, but that a broader view is needed, encompassing the indirect impacts of evaluation upon power relations and upon the knowledge basis on which decision-making relies.

Ryan, K. E. (2005) 'Making educational accountability more democratic', *American Journal of Evaluation*, vol 26, no 4, pp532–543

Educational accountability is a fundamental right of citizens in a democratic society serving the public interest. The US No Child Left Behind Act of 2001 holds states, school districts, public officials, educators, parents and students accountable through auditable performance standards. At the same time, the lack of discussion about how to decide what educational outcomes should be typifies a climate of control. This article proposes making educational accountability more democratic by constructing democratic accountability within the context of a local school and/or district as a democratic conversation. The foundations of democratic accountability, the meaning of democratic accountability and how its meaning is constructed (including accountability for what, to whom and how it is implemented) are outlined.

4.6 EMPOWERMENT EVALUATION

Exemplary evaluation questions relating to empowerment evaluation

- How can policy-makers and other stakeholders involved be assisted in self-evaluation?
- In particular, how can those stakeholders who encounter difficulty in accessing policy-making and policy evaluation be endorsed and empowered to gain entrance and become involved?

4.6.1 Elucidation and context

The essence of the method

What?

Empowerment evaluation 'is designed to help people help themselves and improve their programmes using a form of self-evaluation and reflection' (Fetterman, 1997, p382). In this approach, policy evaluation is not so much a goal as a means of allowing individuals, groups and coalitions involved in policy evaluation to achieve self-realization and self-development.

Fetterman, the founder of the method, asserts that empowerment evaluation stands for 'the use of evaluation concepts and techniques to foster self-determination'. Self-determination is described as the capacity to chart one's own course by:

- determining and making known one's needs;
- setting goals;
- outlining a plan of approach;
- finding the means;
- making choices between various alternatives;
- taking strides towards goal attainment;
- ascertaining whether short- and medium-term goals are being achieved;
- persevering in striving for goal attainment.

Empowerment evaluation, by definition, is a method applied to a group. This group includes policy-makers (from the public authorities), as well as members of the policy target group. As a group, agreement is reached on the objectives to be realized, the strategies to be deployed to this end, and the products to be delivered in order to achieve goal attainment.

Fetterman (1997) asserts that his approach complements the traditional evaluation methods, which, according to him, have a weakness in that they assess a policy programme at a given moment (i.e. they provide a snapshot). In his approach, the focus is on evolutions in policy-making. Consequently, empowerment evaluation offers the advantage that processes of self-evaluation are institutionalized in policy-making. Therefore, policy-makers are better able to respond to changes in the policy context.

When?
Although this approach can be applied in outlining and introducing policy (with group decisions on interim goals to be achieved), empowerment evaluation is used mainly for assessing policy programmes in their implementation phase. The approach may be *ex ante*, *ex nunc* or *ex post*.

Advantages and disadvantages?
Empowerment evaluation offers at least two advantages:

1 First, it is an evaluation method that is applied to groups. All parties involved are given an opportunity to express their views on their own functioning and the policy that is being pursued. Colleagues, the evaluator and other interested parties are able to respond to one another's statements. In this way, a common vision is developed, which, under the impulse of all participants' contributions, is constantly called into question, corrected or confirmed. Thus, a subsystem of checks and balances is incorporated within empowerment evaluation.
2 Another strength of empowerment evaluation is that it is a continuous process, where the evolution of policy is monitored in a group. In this way, self-evaluation is institutionalized in policy-making.

There are also a number of important disadvantages to empowerment evaluation:

• Critics have pointed out that there is a degree of overlap between empowerment evaluation and other participatory approaches, such as utilization-focused evaluation. This approach, too, is about ownership, application-oriented assessment, developing insight into one's own situation, involvement and capacity-building. Still, according to these critics, the champions of empowerment evaluation have thus far not succeeded in providing adequate arguments for the thesis that empowerment evaluation is structurally different from such other approaches. Conceptual vagueness still needs to be resolved, including in relation to where participation ends and empowerment begins.
• Furthermore, the proponents of empowerment evaluation seem to suggest that it is more important to empower than it is to arrive at correct evaluative conclusions. Critics of the approach argue that there is a danger of people directly involved in policy-making coming too close to the object of evaluation, resulting in inevitable bias in the evaluative conclusions reached.

It is often to the benefit of professional policy implementers not to be too critical about their own performances as their employment may depend upon it.

Historical context

Fetterman outlined the principles of empowerment evaluation in 1993, the year in which he chaired the American Evaluation Association (AEA). The topic of that year's AEA convention was empowerment evaluation. The ideas that were launched on that occasion were subsequently complemented and specified in various publications. In 1995, Fetterman won the Alva and Gunnar Mydral Award for Evaluation Practice. The recipient in 1996 was Shakeh Kaftarian. Both authors won the award for their contributions on empowerment evaluation.

Research and evaluation context

Empowerment evaluation, like deliberative democratic evaluation (see Section 4.5), responsive evaluation (see Section 4.10), utilization-focused evaluation (see Section 4.11) and constructivist evaluation (see Section 4.4), attaches great importance to the participation of the various stakeholders. These participatory or interactive approaches to policy evaluation involve knowledge input by practical and experiential experts because such knowledge can be very useful in gaining a better understanding of policy practice and in formulating relevant and practicable policy recommendations. Empowerment evaluation does, however, adopt a different emphasis than the other participatory methods. It devotes closer attention to the self-development and self-realization of participants.

4.6.2 Methodology

Steps in empowerment evaluation

Four steps need to be taken in order to help others evaluate their policy programmes:

1 Take stock of the situation.
2 Set goals.
3 Develop strategies.
4 Document progress.

Taking stock of the situation

Participants in the evaluation project are requested to attribute a score to their policy programme ranging from 1 to 10, with 10 the best score. They should provide a general appreciation, as well as an appreciation of specific aspects of policy. The participants are also asked to explain the scores attributed. This technique is used to determine how far the implementation of the policy project has progressed and to identify strengths and weaknesses in policy implementation.

Setting goals

Participants in the evaluation study are asked to specify which score the policy programme ought to attain in the future. Subsequently, they are asked which goals ought to be attained in order to achieve that score. These goals must be determined in consultation with the evaluator in order to ensure that they are relevant and feasible. It is important that the interim goals should take into account not only the final goals, but also the personal assets of those involved, their competencies, available finances, etc.

Developing strategies

Participants in the evaluation project are made responsible for searching for and developing strategies in order to achieve the set goals. In this phase, brainstorming, critical debate and techniques for reaching consensus and drawing conclusions are emphasized. Policy strategies are scrutinized on a regular basis in order to evaluate their efficiency and appropriateness. The strategies are determined consultatively by policy-makers, policy implementers and the representatives of the target group.

Documenting progress

In the fourth step, the participants in the evaluation project are asked which type of documentation will be required to monitor progress in their work. This is a crucial step in the evaluation process. Each indicator is screened for relevance in order to avoid time being wasted on collecting data that is not useful or is vague. The participants in the evaluation project are asked to elucidate the connection between the indicators and the policy goal. The information collected should be credible and accurate.

Remarks

Usually, an internal (government) evaluator will conduct the evaluation study. The evaluator is on an equal footing with the project participants. He fulfils the role of the critical friend who questions the prevailing perceptions within the group. He shows them how to evaluate the progress made towards the attainment of the (individual, self-set) goals and how to modify their plans and strategies on the basis of this evaluation.

Empowerment evaluation involves qualitative as well as quantitative techniques.

References and Examples

Primary and additional references

Fetterman, D. M. (1997) 'Empowerment evaluation and accreditation in higher education', in E. Chelimsky and W. R. Shadish (eds) *Evaluation for the 21st Century: A Handbook*, Sage, Thousand Oaks, CA

Fetterman, D. M. (2001) *Foundations of Empowerment Evaluation*, Sage, Thousand Oaks, CA

Fetterman, D. M. and Wandersman, A. (2004) *Empowerment Evaluation Principles in Practice*, Guilford Press, New York, NY

Fetterman, D. and Wandersman, A. (2007) 'Empowerment evaluation: Yesterday, today, and tomorrow', *American Journal of Evaluation*, vol 28, no 2, pp179–198

Fetterman, D. M., Kaftarian, S. J. and Wandersman, A. (1996) *Empowerment Evaluation: Knowledge and Tools for Self-Assessment and Accountability*, Sage, Thousand Oaks, CA

Smith, N. L. (2007) 'Empowerment evaluation as evaluation ideology', *American Journal of Evaluation*, vol 28, no 2, pp169–178

Examples

Miller, R. L. and Campbell, R. (2006) 'Taking stock of empowerment evaluation, an empirical review', *American Journal of Evaluation*, vol 27, no 3, pp296–319

The authors systematically examined 47 case examples of empowerment evaluation published from 1994 through June 2005. The results suggest wide variation among practitioners in adherence to empowerment evaluation principles and weak emphasis on the attainment of empowered outcomes for programme beneficiaries. Implications for theory and practice are discussed.

Chambers, J. M., Schnoes, C. J. and Murphy-Berman, V. (2000) 'Empowerment evaluation applied: Experiences, analysis, and recommendations from a case study', *American Journal of Evaluation*, vol 21, no 1, pp53–64

The empowerment evaluation approach is applied and examined within the context of a case study involving three comprehensive communities' initiatives, aiming to meet the needs of children and families in communities. In this article, the authors discuss, from both theoretical and empirical perspectives, issues related to the evaluator's role, differences relative to other inclusive evaluation approaches, stakeholder involvement, evaluation context variables, and the concept and practice of empowering programme participants via an evaluation approach.

4.7 EVALUABILITY ASSESSMENT

Exemplary evaluation questions relating to evaluability assessment

- Is there a societal and/or political demand for evaluation, and with whom?
- Are the agencies in the policy domain concerned willing to be the object of an evaluation study?
- Are we in the political and practical circumstances to conduct a policy evaluation?

4.7.1 Elucidation and context

The essence of the method

What?

An evaluability assessment (EA) is made prior to an evaluation as a kind of pre-evaluation reality check. Its purpose is to establish whether a project or policy can be evaluated and which barriers might exist to an effective and useful evaluation.

An evaluability assessment encompasses a number of elements:

- an analysis of the coherence and logic of an intervention;
- clarification with regard to the availability of data;
- assessment of the extent to which the administration and target groups have the intention of using the evaluation outcomes (given the presence or absence of interest and the state of affairs in the policy process).

The following questions are central to an evaluability assessment:

- Should policy be evaluated?
- How should it be evaluated?
- Which evaluation approach should be taken?
- Which purpose should the evaluation study serve (for policy-makers and target groups)?

Evaluability assessment provides for:

- a clear statement of the policy goals;
- the identification of indicators to measure policy performance;
- the determination of options in order to improve the quality of policy-making.

According to Wholey (1979, pxiii), the founder of the approach, evaluability assessment is about the following:

Evaluability assessment explores the objectives, expectations and information needs of programme managers and policy-makers; explores programme reality; assesses the likelihood that programme activities will achieve measurable progress toward programme objectives; and assesses the extent to which evaluation information is likely to be used by programme management. The products of evaluability assessment are:

1 *a set of agreed-on programme objectives, side effects and performance indicators on which the programme can realistically be held accountable; and*

2 *a set of evaluation/management options that represent ways in which management can change programme activities, objectives or uses of information in ways likely to improve* programme performance.

When?

An evaluability assessment is carried out after an *ex ante* evaluation (in which policy options are weighed up), but before an *ex nunc* evaluation of policy implementation. Conducting an evaluability assessment at an early stage of the policy process can help to elucidate the logic of policy interventions and lead to policy improvements before the process has reached too advanced a stage to make such modifications.

Advantages and disadvantages?

Evaluability assessment offers the advantage that it can serve various purposes:

- An EA is conducted first and foremost to establish whether it makes sense to carry out an extensive evaluation study of a particular policy programme.
- An evaluability assessment may also be carried out to clarify the premises of policy: the underlying goals, means and expectations are all laid bare.
- A third, rather more ambitious, purpose of evaluability assessment may be to arrive at recommendations regarding necessary modifications to the policy design. In this sense, the method can serve as a policy adjustment tool.

In conducting an evaluability assessment, there are three commonly occurring problems:

1 The first is related to the fact that an evaluability assessment is a group activity. The ideal working group for an evaluability assessment should be composed of representatives of the policy target group, policy-makers (high-ranked civil servants, cabinet staff and/or politicians) and policy implementers. This guarantees that a broad range of stakeholders and interested parties is

represented so that they can develop a common view on the policy initiative. If the group does not function properly, then the credibility of the evaluation project may suffer and the study may be a waste of money. Ensuring that the group is coherent from the start of the evaluation is essential in order for the study to be productive and efficient.

2 The second problem with evaluability assessment is that it is time consuming. Much time is invested in the recruitment of staff, the collection of documentation and the resolution of conflicts. Detailed planning, the appropriate distribution of tasks and the provision of leadership for all assignments and activities are good strategies in order to control the time that needs to be spent on the evaluability assessment.

3 A third problem is that, in practice, evaluability assessment often does not lead to a fully fledged evaluation study. Evaluability assessment frequently provides clues as to the remediation of shortcomings in policy. The method is applied, for example, to make explicit and clarify the goals of policy (in situations where they are either absent, or vague or ambiguous) or for aligning conflicting views of stakeholders.

Historical context

The most detailed approach to evaluability assessment was developed during the early 1970s by a research group at the Urban Institute in Washington, DC. The impetus for developing the method was twofold:

1 First, the US had experienced a boom in evaluation research methods during the 1960s. Evaluation projects were implemented in a whole range of policy domains and public services. However, it became clear comparatively quickly that these studies yielded little useful information for policy-makers and implementers alike. Some began to doubt whether evaluation projects had any value added to offer and called into question whether such studies were worth spending money on.

2 The evaluators, too, were dissatisfied. Policy initiatives often lacked any official statement of goals or they had goals that were irrelevant or impossible to measure. Quite often, policy also lacked a clear rationale with regard to the means deployed in light of the goals to be achieved. Moreover, some policy programmes appeared to be immune to critical evaluation as policy would not be modified for political or ideological reasons.

In response to these issues, Wholey (1979) put forward the notion of evaluability assessment as a procedure for determining whether policy initiatives were ready for evaluation. Since then, the approach has been further developed by others (including Smith, 1989, and Rog, 1985). It is an approach that is known primarily in the US, but which has been applied increasingly rarely since the mid

1980s. According to Smith (1989), this is due to the fact that the pioneer of the method (i.e. Wholey) no longer conducts projects on behalf of the US federal administration. However, some prominent evaluators maintain that evaluability assessment is an essential evaluation approach.

Research and evaluation context

Evaluability assessment belongs to the group of *clarificative evaluation approaches*. These approaches focus on the clarification of the internal structure and functioning of policy. In clarificative evaluation, policy programmes are described, programme theory is studied, policy design is assessed for workability, policy on paper and policy in practice are compared, and a foundation is laid for monitoring policy implementation and effects.

4.7.2 Methodology

Steps in evaluability assessment

Smith (1989) has developed a step-by-step approach that can serve as a guideline in making an evaluability assessment. The approach does not follow a fixed pattern: depending upon the context and the objectives of the evaluation, certain steps may be omitted or their order may be switched. Smith (1989) distinguishes nine steps:

1 Determine the purpose, secure commitment and identify work group members.
2 Define the boundaries of the policy programme.
3 Identify and analyse programme documents.
4 Develop/clarify policy programme theory.
5 Identify and interview stakeholders and describe their attitudes towards policy.
6 Identify stakeholder needs, concerns and differences in perceptions of the policy programme.
7 Determine the plausibility of the programme theory.
8 Draw conclusions and formulate recommendations.
9 Plan specific steps for using evaluability assessment data.

Determine the purpose, secure commitment and identify work group members
A clearly articulated purpose will foster commitment on the part of stakeholders. The work group should ideally consist of seven to nine members representing important stakeholder groups and policy programme administrators.

Define the boundaries of the policy programme to be studied
This step will:

1   delimit the policy initiative to be evaluated;
2   clarify the purpose of the EA; and
3   determine the role that the work group will play.

Identify and analyse programme documents
The documents should pertain to the original intent of the policy initiative and policy implementation. The analysis should, among other things, provide insight into underlying politics of the policy programme.

Develop/clarify policy programme theory
A policy programme is always based on a logic regarding the deployment of certain means coupled with the realization of certain policy goals. Identifying the assumptions underlying policy, the available resources, policy programme activities and objectives, as well as how these components relate to one another are key elements in analysing a programme theory.

Identify and interview stakeholders and describe their attitudes towards policy
Stakeholders should be allowed to elucidate how they perceive the policy initiative. Interviews should be taken that focus on what exactly stakeholders know about the content of policy and the mechanisms behind it.

Identify stakeholder needs, concerns and differences in perception of the policy programme
Differences in needs, concerns and perceptions can be an indication of misconceptions with regard to policy and its intent, or they may signify that policy is inadequately meeting the needs of one or more stakeholder groups.

Determine the plausibility of the programme theory
Data from policy-makers, documentation and stakeholder interviews are used to determine the plausibility of the programme theory. On the basis of the available data, the policy theory may be adjusted if required.

Draw conclusions and formulate recommendations
The EA team draws conclusions and formulates recommendations. Conclusions and recommendations are based on the data collected.

Plan specific steps for using evaluability assessment data

The subsequent step may be to continue with a further evaluation of the policy programme, to revise/terminate the policy programme, or to decide that no action is to be taken.

References and Examples

Primary and additional references

Nay, J. N. and Kay, P. (1982) *Government Oversight and Evaluability Assessment*, Lexington Books, Lexington, MA

Rog, D. (1985) *A Methodological Analysis of Evaluability Assessment*, PhD thesis, Vanderbilt University at Nashville, TN

Rutman, L. (1980) *Planning Useful Evaluations*, Sage, Beverly Hills, CA

Smith, M. F. (1989) *Evaluability Assessment: A Practical Approach*, Kluwer Academic Publishers, Clemson, NC

Trevisan, M. S. and Huang Y. M. (2003) 'Evaluability assessment: A primer', *Practical Assessment, Research and Evaluation*, vol 8, no 20, http://PAREonline. net/getvn.asp? v=8&n=20, accessed 1 March 2008

Wholey, J. S. (1979) *Evaluation: Promise and Performance*, The Urban Institute, Washington, DC

Examples

Smith has conducted several evaluability assessments, including of a water quality/quantity programme in Maryland, in the US. Smith (1989) refers to this example in the work referred to above.

Trevisan, M. S. (2007) 'Evaluability assessment from 1986 to 2006', *American Journal of Evaluation*, vol 28, no 3, pp290–303

This article presents the state of practice of evaluability assessment as represented in the published literature from 1986 to 2006. Twenty-three EA studies were located, showing that EA was conducted in a wide variety of programmes, disciplines and settings. The findings suggest that EA is practised and published more widely than previously known.

Snodgrass, D. and Woller, G. (2006) 'Evaluability assessment of PROFIT Zambia', www.microlinks.org/ev_en.php?ID=13089_201&ID2=DO_TOPIC, accessed 1 March 2008

This evaluability assessment was completed prior to embarking on an impact assessment of the PROFIT Zambia programme. The document assesses the causal model underlying the programme, the appropriateness of programme design in light of its causal model, the programme timeframe, and other programme characteristics. The results of the analysis are used to determine the appropriateness of conducting an impact assessment of the programme and, if so, what the design/methodology of the impact assessment should be.

4.8 META-EVALUATION AND META-ANALYSIS

Exemplary evaluation question relating to meta-evaluation and meta-analysis

- How should evaluation studies, evaluation systems or evaluation tools themselves be evaluated?

4.8.1 Elucidation and context

The essence of the approach

What?

There are two types of meta-evaluation/analysis (MEA):

1   In the first sense of the word, meta-evaluation/analysis is a method for making an evaluation on the basis of other studies and evaluations. Evaluation studies of this type are often quantitative in nature; but reutilization of data is also possible with qualitative studies/evaluations. This type of meta-study is often referred to as meta-analysis.
2   In the second sense, the term refers to the evaluation of evaluation studies. In other words, an existing evaluation is evaluated on the basis of a number of criteria. The evaluation may be assessed in its entirety or per component. These components may be goals, the object, the process or the effects of the evaluation. Hereafter, we call this form of MEA meta-evaluation.

When?

MEA, in both senses, uses as its input the outcomes of other studies. Consequently, an MEA can only take place when sufficient other research or evaluations have been carried out.

With regard to the phase of the policy cycle in which MEA can be conducted, the evaluator and his/her client enjoy freedom of choice. The likelihood that a whole series of studies has been carried out *ex ante* is rather small. Therefore, MEA usually takes an *ex post* approach (i.e. after implementation and evaluation of policy).

Advantages and disadvantages?

The most significant advantage of *meta-analysis* is that it involves few or even no operational costs. It is an entirely intellectual endeavour that requires no expensive research techniques such as surveys or focus groups and interviews. The greatest disadvantage of meta-analysis is that one has to rely upon the supply of data from the 'source evaluations'. The evaluator has no impact upon previous evaluations and can therefore not steer or direct the research questions, methods and techniques. The evaluator must simply use the material that is available to him or her.

One of the merits of *meta-evaluation* is that it offers a critical view of evaluations. In this way, it provides a kind of quality control on the work of evaluators. On the other hand, meta-evaluation gives rise to another quality control issue: who should evaluate the quality of the meta-evaluation?

Historical context

Scriven first used the term *meta-evaluation* in 1969. During the course of the 1970s, MEA began to attract more and more interest. Scriven and Stufflebeam both devoted a great deal of attention to the method. Their interest in MEA stemmed from their critical view on evaluations. They ascertained that, despite the boom of the 1960s, evaluations had not always had the required policy relevance. They tried to explain this by assessing the evaluations critically – in other words, by making evaluations of the evaluations.

Research and evaluation context

Both meta-evaluation and meta-analysis are relevant to policy evaluation. In the sense of meta-analysis, or the use of various other evaluations for the purpose of conducting one's own evaluation, MEA has an important application in situations where the evaluation budget is limited or where the evaluator has a preference for the (re)use of quantitative data.

Meta-analysis is a form of *comparative case study research*. Initially, it was used for the evaluation of (semi-)controlled experiments. Later, the field of application was extended to quantitative evaluations.

Since meta-evaluation is an evaluation of other evaluations, it occupies a special position in the field of evaluation. By means of a meta-evaluation, one can assess the adequacy, the usability and the cost-effectiveness of other evaluations.

4.8.2 Methodology

Steps in meta-evaluation and meta-analysis

In what follows, we present two step-by-step approaches: one for meta-analysis, the other for meta-evaluation.

Meta-analysis (evaluation based on other evaluations)

Meta-analysis is comprised of eight consecutive steps:

1 *Specify the object and topic area.* This first step provides more information on the object and topic to be evaluated. This involves an explicit specification of the principles, the evaluation questions posed, relevant variables, target groups, stakeholders and possibly other influential factors.

2 *Specify the evaluation strategy.* Here, the evaluator specifies which sources should be taken into account in the search for appropriate evaluations to incorporate within the meta-analysis.

3 *Develop criteria for selecting the evaluations to be used.* Once the sources for evaluations have been determined, the evaluator needs to decide on selection criteria. On the basis of these selection criteria, the evaluator will choose which evaluations are to be used.

4 *Calculate the size of the effects, code the estimated size and compute the deviations.* In this step, the evaluator gains an idea of the order of magnitude of the dispersion of effects (effect size) in the various evaluations. The intention is, after all, to combine effects as found in the previous studies. By coding the effects on the basis of size and dispersion, they can also be combined and used in the following steps.

5 *Develop a scheme for coding evaluation studies and their properties, and test for suitability.* The collection of evaluations needs to be ordered. To this end, the evaluator must develop a coding system. Boruch and Petrosino (2004) suggest that one should opt for two independent encoders (*double coding*) in order to enhance reliability. Since the processing happens statistically, one needs to pay attention to the coding technique. Most handbooks on the statistical processing of research data provide an explanation of how this should be done under the heading 'Effect size statistics'.

6 *Develop a management strategy and procedures for the meta-analysis.* Although evaluation management and evaluation procedure in a meta-analysis are no different than in other evaluation procedures, it is important that we should mention this step. It is here that attention is paid to aspects such as staff allocation and planning the meta-analysis.

7 *Develop an analysis strategy.* The seventh step is the actual analysis of all the data. In order for the analysis to be successful, one first needs to develop a good analysis strategy. To this end, the evaluator should order all of the data at his/her disposal. Then he should study the (policy) effect.

8 *Interpret and report the results.* The previous step yielded analysis data that need to be interpreted in order to arrive at an assessment or evaluation. Isolated results of statistical operations are inadequate for drawing evaluative conclusions. In other words, they need to be interpreted. This interpretation together with the statistical argument presented in the analysis are incorporated within the evaluation report.

Meta-evaluation (evaluation of the evaluation)
According to Stufflebeam (1974), a meta-evaluation consists of three steps:

1 *Specification of the data requirements.* The evaluator determines which aspect of the primary evaluation (i.e. the evaluation to be evaluated) will be assessed. Here, a choice can be made between the goals, the topic, the process or the effects of the evaluation. Depending upon the choice made, a need arises for a specific type of data on the evaluation.
2 *Data collection.* In order to satisfy the need for information, the relevant data need to be collected. Here, the evaluator must take into account the evaluation criteria to be applied to the primary evaluation.

   Stufflebeam (1974) proposes 11 such criteria:

   i   *Internal validity:* this criterion concerns the extent to which the findings are true.
   ii *External validity:* how general is the information?
   iii *Reliability:* how accurate is the data?
   iv *Objectivity:* this criterion deals with the public nature of the data. Would everyone interpret the data in this way or is the interpretation dependent upon the evaluator's personal experience?
   v   *Relevance:* do the results correspond with the expectations of policy-makers vis-à-vis the evaluation?
   vi *Importance:* have the most important aspects been studied?
   vii *Scope:* has the evaluation answered all of the audience's important questions?
   viii *Credibility:* is the evaluator free of bias in the eyes of the audience?
   ix *Timeliness:* was the evaluation carried out in time to serve its purpose?
   x   *Pervasiveness:* the utility of the evaluation depends largely upon whether the intended audiences have received and used the findings.
   xi *Cost-effectiveness:* does the effectiveness of the evaluation outweigh its cost?

3 *Data utilization.* Once the data have been collected, the evaluator may test the selected aspects of the evaluation for the above criteria.

References and Examples

Primary and additional references

Boruch, R. and Petrosino, A. (2004) 'Meta-analysis, systematic reviews, and research syntheses', in J. S. Wholey, H. P. Hatry and K. E. Newcomer (eds) *Handbook of Practical Program Evaluation*, Wiley, San Francisco, CA
Lincoln, Y. and Guba, E. (1985) *Naturalistic Inquiry*, Sage, Beverly Hills, CA

Patton, M. Q. (1990) *Qualitative Evaluation and Research Methods*, Sage, Newbury Park, CA

Scriven, M. (1969) 'An introduction to meta-evaluation', *Educational Product Report*, vol 2, no 5, pp36–38

Stufflebeam, D. L. (1974) 'Meta-evaluation', Paper 3 in the Occasional Paper Series, www.wmich.edu/evalctr/pubs/ops/ops03.pdf, accessed 1 March 2008

Stufflebeam, D. L. (2001) 'Evaluation models', *New Directions for Evaluation*, no 89

Examples

Oltmer, K., Nijkamp, P., Florax, R. and Brouwer, F. (2000), 'A meta-analysis of environmental impacts of agri-environmental policies in the European Union', Discussion paper, Tinbergen Institute, Amsterdam/Rotterdam, The Netherlands, www.tinbergen.nl/discussionpapers/00083.pdf, accessed 1 March 2008

This paper applies a meta-analysis to the evaluation of agri-environmental policy in the European Union. Statistical analysis of previous research results is reused. The paper investigates whether specific conditions, under which agri-environmental measures are applied, have an effect on the behaviour of farmers with respect to three indicators: nitrogen fertilizer, livestock density and area of grassland. The results indicate that agri-environmental policy intervention has a positive effect on the behaviour of farmers participating in agri-environmental programmes.

Universalia (2000) 'IUCN meta-evaluation: An analysis of IUCN evaluations 1994-2000', www.iucn.org/programme/eval/documents2/meta_evaluation_00.pdf, accessed 1 March 2008

The World Conservation Union (IUCN) – formerly the International Union for the Conservation of Nature – is a global environmental non-governmental organization (NGO). Universalia, a team of consultants, was commissioned to conduct a meta-analysis of evaluations commissioned by the IUCN from 1994 to 2000. Universalia examined 93 evaluation reports concerning biodiversity, forests, marine and coastal areas, natural resource management, water resources, etc. to assess the quality and scope of IUCN evaluations. Based on this assessment, a set of 13 major findings were described.

Banerjee, A. and Solomon, B. D. (2003) 'Eco-labeling for energy efficiency and sustainability: A meta-evaluation of US programs', *Energy Policy*, vol 31, no 2, pp109–123

Eco-labeling is a market-based approach for improving the environmental performance of products through consumer choice. This article evaluates five US energy-labelling programmes by employing existing evaluation studies. The authors used two evaluation criteria: consumer response and manufacturer/marketer response. It was found that government programmes were much more successful than private programmes.

4.9 MIXED-METHOD EVALUATION

Exemplary evaluation question relating to mixed-method evaluation
- How should one carry out a policy evaluation when applying a broad mix of analysis techniques?

4.9.1 Elucidation and context

The essence of the approach

What?

In mixed-method evaluation (MME), quantitative and qualitative methods are combined. Quantitative methods are research methods dealing with numerical data and anything measurable. Qualitative methods are research methods in which no numerical material is used, but other types of data are. Qualitative data result in explanatory descriptions of a situation, while quantitative data result in a calculative description. MME combines the two approaches for the purpose of directing and evaluating policy programmes; once they have exerted an effect, MME assesses their effectiveness (Stufflebeam, 2001).

When?

MME is not restricted to a particular phase of the policy or evaluation cycle. It is a broadly applicable method that is primarily used for: evaluations in a complex context and evaluations in which a multitude of questions need to be answered.

According to Stufflebeam (2001), the purpose of MME is to assess the effectiveness of policy programmes and, on this basis, to modify, if necessary. For this reason, Stufflebeam feels that MME is best carried out *ex post*, after the effects have manifested themselves. Nevertheless, the combination of quantitative and qualitative data may also be applied in *ex ante* evaluations, before policy has been implemented.

Advantages and disadvantages?

MME has the following strengths:

- It uses both qualitative and quantitative methods so that it provides a more comprehensive and precise picture of the object of research than methods that are exclusively qualitative or quantitative in nature.
- MME enhances the reliability and validity of the research findings by applying different methodologies.

The method also has a number of weaknesses:

- MME insists on the use of both qualitative and quantitative data. Depending upon the evaluation questions to be answered, however, it may be more appropriate to apply either one or the other.
- MME is sometimes applied to cover up the lack of fine detail in individual (quantitative or qualitative) methods. This is something the client, in particular, should be wary of.

Historical context

One of the pioneers of mixed method evaluation is Tyler (1932). Tyler was the first to realize the strengths and weaknesses of the method and to apply the approach in practice. Guba, Lincoln and Patton, all of whom are renowned contemporary evaluators, have contributed to developing MME into a recognized evaluation approach. In their own work, they have also emphasized the importance of using quantitative as well as qualitative data.

Research and evaluation context

MME provides formal confirmation of an academic consensus on the significance of both quantitative and qualitative data in scientific (evaluation) research. It used to be the case that some evaluators swore by quantitative data, while others made the argument for qualitative information. By the mid 1970s, after a veritable titanic struggle between the two perspectives, academic circles came to accept that a combination of qualitative and quantitative data provides a richer and more effective evaluation than either of the one-sided approaches.

Meanwhile, MME has come to be seen as confirmation of the long-established tradition of combining qualitative and quantitative methods in evaluation studies. In this sense, MME is no longer exceptional or new (National Science Foundation, 1997).

4.9.2 Methodology

Steps in mixed-method evaluation

We distinguish five steps in the application of MME:

1 formulating the evaluation questions;
2 choosing a data collection method;
3 data collection;
4 data analysis;
5 reporting.

Formulating the evaluation questions

This step consists of four elements:

1   Clarify the purpose of the evaluation project.
2   Identify stakeholder and target groups.
3   Sum up, order and rank evaluation questions per target group.
4   Choose between the various evaluation questions, given the available resources.

The *User-Friendly Handbook for Project Evaluation* (National Science Foundation, 1997) contains a checklist to help the evaluator run through these steps.

Choosing a data collection method

This step addresses three key research questions:

1   Which collection method is the most appropriate for this type of data?
2   How can the available data, originating from different sources, be combined most effectively?
3   Which method fits into the available budget?

It is important that one should devise a data collection and combination plan beforehand. Since this involves several considerations, one is likely to have to compromise to a certain extent.

Data collection

There are a number of focal points to take into account in relation to data collection:

- timing of the data collection;
- sampling;
- choice regarding the order of data collection;
- frequency with which data should be collected;
- costs of data collection.

The *User-Friendly Handbook for Project Evaluation* (National Science Foundation, 1997) suggests that a timeline should be put forward for data collection, data analysis and reporting. In the third step, more practical and organizational arrangements are made.

Data analysis

Data analysis modalities are highly dependent upon the method selected and the manner in which the collected data are integrated. In this respect, the evaluator should decide what is the most appropriate approach.

Reporting

The report concludes and assesses the evaluation. In this context, attention should be paid to the following aspects:

- due account of the needs of the target group;
- composition of the final report;
- clear formulation of conclusions and recommendations;
- any non-disclosure agreements made to be respected.

References and Examples

Primary and additional references

Johnson, R. B., Onwuegbuzie, A. J. and Turner, L. A. (2007) 'Toward a definition of mixed methods research', *Journal of Mixed Methods Research*, vol 1, no 2, pp112–133

Lincoln, Y. and Guba, E. (1985) *Naturalistic Inquiry*, Sage, Beverly Hills, CA

National Science Foundation (1997) *User-Friendly Handbook for Mixed Method Evaluation: Science, Mathematics, Engineering, and Technical Education*, National Science Foundation, Washington, DC, www.ehr.nsf.gov/EHR/REC/pubs/NSF97-153/start.htm, accessed 1 March 2008

Patton, M. Q. (2001) *Qualitative Evaluation and Research Methods*, Sage, Newbury Park, CA

Stufflebeam, D. L. (2001) 'Evaluation models', *New Directions for Evaluation*, no 89

Examples

MacKay, K. J. and Campbell, M. (2004) 'A mixed method approach for measuring environmental impacts in nature-based tourism and outdoor recreation settings', *Tourism Analysis*, vol 9, no 3, pp141–152

The example provided in this article examined abiotic, biotic and cultural (social) dimensions of tourism and recreation impacts in Riding Mountain National Park, Manitoba, Canada, using a mixed-method approach. The study demonstrates how biophysical and socio-cultural research methods can be systematically employed to expand traditional impact monitoring and assessment models and, consequently, to advance understanding of recreation and tourism impacts upon the environment through an integrated interpretation of the results.

Dunning, H., Williams, A., Abonyi, S. and Crooks, V. (2008), 'A mixed method approach to quality of life research: A case study approach', *Social Indicators Research*, vol 85, no 1, pp145–158

Quality of life is defined as an interdisciplinary topic of investigation that emerged as a focus of geographic enquiry during the 1970s, when researchers sought to understand social problems arising from social and economic inequities. The authors of this article examine how to work effectively within a mixed method framework in quality-of-life research. Data from the Community–University Institute for Social Research Quality of Life project in Saskatoon, Canada, are used for operationalization. The article presents seven benefits and four guidelines.

4.10 RESPONSIVE EVALUATION

Exemplary evaluation question relating to responsive evaluation

- How to organize an evaluation in which the stakeholders assist the evaluator in the selection of topics and criteria, as well as in searching for solutions to the problems revealed by the evaluation?

4.10.1 Elucidation and context

The essence of the method

What?

Responsive evaluation was developed during the early 1970s by Stake, an expert in the evaluation of education policy who worked at the University of Illinois, US. Stake called his evaluation approach responsive because stakeholders are involved in selecting the methods to be applied in the evaluation study.

In defining responsive evaluation, Stake asserts that an evaluation is responsive 'if it orients more directly to programme activities than to programme intents; responds to audience requirements for information; and if the different value perspectives present are referred to in reporting the success and failure of the programme' (cited in Worthen, 1997, p159).

Stake emphasizes that it is more important to take into account the reality of the policy programme than to consider the formal planning and goals of the policy in question.

Characteristic of the approach is the intent to deal with issues that are deemed essential by those involved in the policy implementation process. Examples that come to mind are organizational difficulties. Such issues are seen as *conceptual organizers* during the evaluation study since they are issues upon which the study especially focuses.

Another essential characteristic of responsive evaluation is that, during the study, the evaluator constantly observes and reports to a group of stakeholders accompanying the evaluation study process. At the start of the evaluation project, he or she will – as soon as feasible – provide feedback to the stakeholders about issues that appear essential on the basis of the initial findings. The evaluator should expect the appraisal to meet with agreement as well as opposition. Subsequently, the evaluator should negotiate issues to be further pursued, select a number of them and then proceed with data collection. In this way, the evaluation design will gradually take shape.

Responsive evaluation aims at identifying the merits and shortcomings of policy. In the evaluation, one takes into account the different and sometimes contradictory criteria of the various interested parties in the policy evaluation. The evaluator concludes on the worth of policy, preceded by an elaborate description of the appraisal by the stakeholders involved. On the basis of the account of the various points of view, the reader should be able to form a knowledgeable opinion.

When?
In principle, responsive evaluation may be applied in any phase of the policy cycle. However, in order for the method to work, it is essential that one is able to reach agreement on selecting issues to be pursued in the evaluation.

Advantages and disadvantages?
Responsive evaluation has at least five strengths:

1   It tries to find answers to evaluation questions posed by the various parties involved in the policy programme under study. The principal stakeholders are, after all, invited to take part.
2   'Responsive evaluation leads to enlightenment of stakeholders' (Owen, 1999, p223–224): stakeholders are adequately informed of the actual characteristics, merits and shortcomings of policy.
3   Responsive evaluation takes into account the changeable nature of policy-making: the evaluation design is adapted to changing circumstances.
4   The approach allows one to show the complexity of social reality. Besides the envisaged policy effects, side effects and coincidental added value are also involved in the evaluation.
5   Responsive evaluation is 'relative': when applying the method, one does not set out in search of an all-embracing conclusion on the policy under evaluation. The approach leaves room for comparing different, often conflicting, opinions of the various stakeholder groups on the data collected.

There are also a number of drawbacks:

•   Responsive evaluation pays (too) much attention to subjective data, such as testimonies. Stake defends his approach by asserting that subjectivity is inherent in every type of observation and measurement. With a view to ascertaining the reliability of the data collected, he formulates the following recommendation: the combination of different techniques of data collection (triangulation), repetition of the study, and the 'operationalization' of abstract concepts. As Stake puts it: 'It is an approach that sacrifices some precision in measurement, hopefully to increase the usefulness of the findings to persons in and around the programme' (cited in Madaus et al, 1986, p292).

- Responsive evaluation is also criticized because the evaluation questions are formulated by the policy implementers, the clients of the evaluator or the evaluation team. While their questions are relevant, they are not the only ones that can be posed. According to Stake, evaluation research should allow room for evaluation questions from the various parties involved. The evaluator must, however, be able to direct these questions so that they are acceptable to all.
- Responsive evaluation needs to unfold in a climate of trust and cooperation between the evaluator and his target group. In circumstances where the (political and/or financial) stakes are high, this condition is often unfulfilled.
- There is a danger that the target group of the evaluation study remains passive so that the evaluator becomes the main (or even the only) actor to make crucial decisions in the evaluation process. Patton (1997, p54) asserts that the fact that 'the stakeholders ... are no more than sources of data and an audience for the evaluation, not real partners in the evaluation process' is a structural weakness of responsive evaluation.

Historical context

Stake pioneered responsive evaluation research. He introduced his approach during the 1970s and it has since been developed further by him and his university colleagues.

Research and evaluation context

According to Stake, responsive evaluation is a formalization of a long-established tradition in informal and intuitive evaluation. Responsive evaluation requires a genial and continuous interaction between the evaluator and those involved in the evaluation process.

Worthen et al (1997) assert that responsive evaluation can be integrated perfectly within other evaluation approaches. In responsive evaluation, the emphasis lies primarily on the problems of the stakeholders, about which the evaluator provides information. Some stakeholders will require information about policy outcomes, while others may want to know which stage has been reached in the (operational) processes, and yet others may be interested in a correct implementation of the policy plans. All of these needs may be fulfilled in responsive evaluation since the approach aims to respond to the different kinds of evaluation questions that the various stakeholders may have.

Responsive evaluation – like empowerment evaluation, deliberative democratic evaluation, utilization-focused evaluation and constructivist evaluation – attaches great importance to the participation of the various stakeholders. These participatory or interactive approaches to policy evaluation involve knowledge input by practical and experiential experts because such knowledge can be very useful in gaining a better understanding of policy practice and in formulating relevant and practicable policy recommendations.

Responsive evaluation differs from the other participatory methods in a number of ways:

- Responsive evaluation differs from *empowerment evaluation* in terms of the role that is attributed to the evaluator. While in the responsive evaluation approach, the evaluator retains control of the evaluation process and cooperates with the stakeholders in trying to attain consensus, in empowerment evaluation, the evaluator relinquishes part of his power to the stakeholders and restricts his or her contribution to a supporting role.
- The difference with *deliberative democratic evaluation* lies in who takes responsibility for the research design. While in responsive evaluation, the research design is shaped, in part, by the stakeholders, in the case of deliberative democratic evaluation, responsibility for the research design is left open.
- *Constructivist evaluation* differs from responsive evaluation in the sense that constructivist evaluation is directed more at creating clarity with regard to the underlying assumptions of policy-making.
- *Utilization-focused evaluation*, more so than responsive evaluation, aims to inform policy-makers on policy review and modifications. Responsive evaluation, on the other hand, is intended first and foremost to encourage group learning.

4.10.2 Methodology

Steps in responsive evaluation

Stake distinguishes 12 elements that are of importance in applying the method. He represents them as the face of a clock (see Figure 4.2). However, while the study begins at the top (at 12 o'clock), it does not necessarily proceed clockwise from then on. During the study, attention shifts from one element to another. In other words, we are not concerned here with sequential phases.

In responsive evaluation, the evaluator begins by drawing up an operational plan in which he or she specifies the data to be collected and the individuals the evaluator intends to negotiate with over the subject and method of research. The evaluator must ensure that several respondents are prepared to follow up on the policy (project) to be evaluated and, if need be, to collect data. With their help, the evaluator describes the policy in a memorandum. It should outline the policy context and discourses, and provide graphs and tables. Subsequently, the evaluator determines what added value the evaluation process might represent to the target group. For this purpose, the evaluator takes stock of the opinions of the

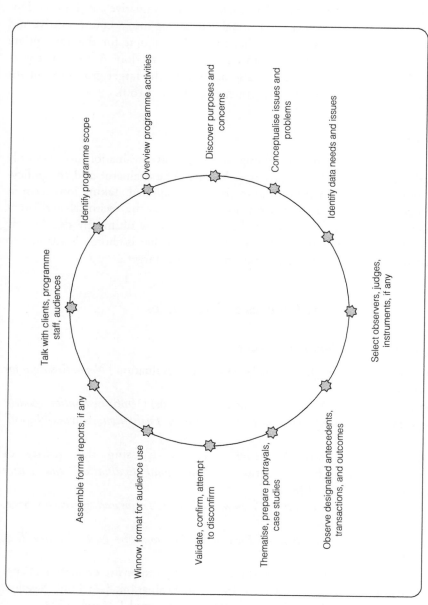

Figure 4.2 *Steps in responsive evaluation*

Source: Stake (cited in Worthen et al, 1997, p161), reproduced by permission of the author and publisher; circle and stars added by Crabbé and Leroy

various parties involved in the policy process. Obviously, he or she must assess the quality of their testimonies. The accuracy of information obtained is subsequently checked by presenting it to policy-makers and implementers. The evaluator asks them to assess the relevance of the first evaluative conclusions. This happens largely in an informal and gradual way, taking into account positive and negative assessments. It is essential that the evaluator opts for the appropriate means of communication in order to encourage interaction. A research report may be the way to go; but one can also agree with the target group to opt for other communication strategies (Worthen et al, 1997, p160).

Remarks

There is a persistent misunderstanding that responsive evaluation involves only qualitative research. This is clearly not the case. The evaluator and the policy-maker must reach agreement on the method to be applied. Taking into account the characteristics of the various methods, as well as the technical and other possibilities of the evaluation team, the evaluator must ultimately decide how data should be collected and analysed. The method that is chosen is adapted to the circumstances and to the evaluation needs of the target group.

References and Examples

Primary and additional references

Abma, T. A. and Greene, J. C. (2002) 'Responsive evaluation', *New Directions for Evaluation*, no 92

Madaus, G. F., Scriven, M. and Stufflebeam, D. L. (eds) (1986) *Evaluation Models: Viewpoints on Educational and Human Services Evaluation*, Kluwer-Nijhoff, Boston, MA

Maxwell, G. S. (1984) 'A rating scale for assessing the quality of responsive/illuminative evaluations', *Educational Evaluation and Policy Analysis*, no 6, pp131–138

Owen, J. M. and Rogers, P. (1999) *Program Evaluation: Forms and Approaches*, Sage, London

Patton, M. Q. (1997) *Utilization-Focused Evaluation: The New Century Text*, Sage, Thousand Oaks, CA

Stake, R. E. (1975) 'Program evaluation, particularly responsive evaluation', Paper presented at a conference on New Trends in Evaluation, Göteborg, Sweden, www.wmich.edu/evalctr/pubs/ops/ops05.html, accessed 1 March 2008

Stake, R. E. (2003) *Standards-Based and Responsive Evaluation*, Sage, New York, NY

Worthen, B. R., Sanders, J. R. and Fitzpatrick, J. L. (1997) *Program Evaluation: Alternative Approaches and Practical Guidelines*, 2nd edition, Longman Publishers, New York, NY

Examples

Abma, T. A. (2006) 'The practice and politics of responsive evaluation', *American Journal of Evaluation*, vol 27, no 1, pp31–43

The author illustrates the practice and politics of responsive evaluation with case examples from two policy fields: arts education and mental healthcare. In these evaluation studies, process-oriented heuristics have been developed to deal with the unequal social relations and power in responsive evaluation. As such, responsive evaluation offers an interesting example of the politics of evaluation. The emerging heuristics may be helpful to other evaluation approaches.

Spiegel, A. N., Bruning, R. H. and Giddings, L. (1999) 'Using responsive evaluation to evaluate a professional conference', *American Journal of Evaluation*, vol 20, no 1, pp57–67

In a statewide conference in Nebraska, US, on alternative methods for assessing students' learning, the researchers incorporated the responsive evaluation method. The application of this method served as a pilot study to illustrate the possible utility of this method in evaluating conferences. This article provides a brief review of the literature surrounding responsive evaluation, a description of the responsive evaluation method applied to this conference, and a discussion of the results and implications of the pilot study.

4.11 UTILIZATION-FOCUSED EVALUATION (U-FE)

Exemplary evaluation questions relating to utilization-focused evaluation

- How can one set up an evaluation that satisfies the knowledge and evaluation needs of policy-makers?
- How can one ensure that the evaluation is aimed specifically at those policy problems to which policy-makers would like to respond?
- How can one maximize the probability that the knowledge gathered and the insights drawn from an evaluation are actually used in (renewed) policy-making?

4.11.1 Elucidation and context

The essence of the method

What?

The ambition of utilization-focused evaluation (UF-E) is to enhance the target-oriented utilization of the evaluation by its target group:

- Utilization-focused evaluation starts from the notion that evaluation studies should be assessed for usability in policy practice.
- In utilization-focused evaluation, one applies values and norms put forward by clearly identified direct users of the evaluation findings (policy-makers, implementers and other stakeholders) who should subsequently take due account of the findings and recommendations.

Underlying utilization-focused evaluation are psychological insights into change processes: the target group will be more inclined to use the evaluation results if it understands the conclusions and feels as if it is the owner of the evaluation process and findings. Its understanding and ownership are stimulated if it is actively involved in the study process. Evaluators should train members of the target group by involving them actively in the evaluation study. In this way, a foundation is laid for implementing the recommendations.

Evaluators should facilitate the evaluation process and design the study in such a way that every step – from the beginning to the end – enhances the usability of the evaluation results. To this end, utilization-focused evaluation does not stand for a specific research approach. U-FE, rather, enhances the *situational responsiveness*, implying that, depending upon the circumstances, a choice is made for a particular research method and techniques. That choice must be a common one; it must be the result of an intense interactive process involving the evaluator and the target group.

When?

Utilization-focused evaluation may be applied at any stage of the policy cycle, but it is most appropriate for *ex post* evaluation of well-defined aspects of policy under implementation.

Advantages and disadvantages?

Utilization-focused evaluation has two big advantages:

1 Maximal policy relevance of the evaluation study is a primary goal in U-FE.
2 U-FE can be perfectly combined with other evaluation methods.

There are also a number of (potential) drawbacks to utilization-focused evaluation:

* The high turnover rate among the target group members is the main limitation of U-FE (Patton, 1997, p380–381). If other people need to be introduced into the work group, one will at least suffer a delay in the study. Staff turnover may also necessitate fresh negotiations over the premises of the evaluation study.
* The approach appears not to be very resilient to abuse on the part of the target group as the latter has so much control over the evaluation study (Stufflebeam, 2001, p79). The target audience has a significant influence on the choice of topic for evaluation, the selection of evaluation questions and the methods to be used. Moreover, it plays an important role in interpreting the (analysed) data, and in deciding whether (or not) one should follow up on the evaluation findings and disseminate them. The stakeholders involved may get caught up in a conflict of interest, which may, in turn, have a profound impact upon the evaluation study.
* It is conceivable that the target group members are unable to make themselves available to monitor the evaluation process intensively. Formulating the most appropriate evaluation questions, making decisions about the evaluation research design, and overseeing data collection and (interim) reflection on evaluative conclusions and their eventual impact is time consuming and requires a considerable effort.

Historical context

The utilization-oriented approach came as a response to the observations that evaluation studies on large-scale government programmes in the US, such as the War on Poverty and Great Society programmes, were having no impact upon public policy (during the 1960s and 1970s). Utilization-focused evaluation responds by putting forward a general framework within which all parties involved can develop a research design more or less jointly in the hope that this will enhance its usability.

Patton (1980, 1982, 1994, 1997, 2008) is the founder of utilization-focused evaluation. Other proponents of the approach are Davis and Salasin (1975), Cronbach et al (1980), the US Joint Committee on Standards for Educational Evaluation (1981, 1994) and Alkin (1995).

Research and evaluation context

Utilization-focused evaluation – like empowerment evaluation, responsive evaluation, deliberative democratic evaluation and constructivist evaluation – attaches great importance to participation by stakeholders. These participatory or interactive approaches to policy evaluation involve knowledge input by practical and experiential experts because such knowledge can be very useful in gaining a better understanding of policy practice and in formulating relevant and practicable policy recommendations.

4.11.2 Methodology

Steps in utilization-focused evaluation

Utilization-focused evaluation encompasses seven steps:

1   Determine the primary intended users.
2   Determine the primary intended uses.
3   Establish evaluation questions.
4   Devise evaluation methods and data collection techniques.
5   Check the interim involvement of primary intended users.
6   Conclude and assess the strategy.
7   Provide a meta-evaluation.

Primary intended users
First, one determines for whom the evaluation is intended. The purpose of this step is to be able to involve those people who have a direct, clearly identifiable, stake in the evaluation. Primary intended users are, in other words, selected and asked to take part in a working group.

Primary intended uses
Within the working groups, the so-called primary intended uses of the evolution study are determined. Consideration is given to how the evaluation study might contribute to policy improvement, to making important policy decisions and to generating knowledge.

Evaluation questions

Together with the evaluator, the members of the working group make decisions on the evaluation questions that the study should address. For each evaluation question, it should be clear which contribution may provide an answer that will help to optimize policy-making.

Evaluation methods and data collection techniques

Next, one discusses the manner in which the evaluation study ought to be conducted. Since the possibilities in evaluation research are so great, it is essential that well-considered choices are made regarding the evaluation method and the manner of data collection. The flowchart depicted in Figure 4.3 shows which crucial considerations need to be made in this context.

Interim involvement of primary intended users

As the data is collected, one needs to check its usability. It makes no sense to collect information that will subsequently turn out to be of no value to policy-making. During the period of data collection, the primary intended users should be informed of the progress being made and of any interim conclusions reached in order to prevent their interest in the study from waning and to ensure the policy relevance of the information gathered. The primary intended users should preferably also be involved in interpreting (analysed) data.

Conclusion and assessment of the strategy

The evaluator then facilitates the use of the evaluative findings by helping to target group members in drawing conclusions and showing them how these conclusions may be applied in policy practice. Together, they draw up an action plan for assessing policy-making. This plan may, together with the analysis, be disseminated to a broader public.

Meta-evaluation

Utilization-focused evaluation ends with an evaluation of the evaluation study (i.e. with a meta-evaluation). One ascertains to what extent planned use is exhibited by the intended users and whether the evaluation has caused any unintended side effects.

Figure 4.3 depicts the steps necessary to execute a utilization-focused evaluation.

Remarks

This approach requires a very competent evaluator who is trusted by the primary intended users. The evaluator must be able to respond flexibly to the circumstances in which he or she is required to conduct the study, while at the same time adhering

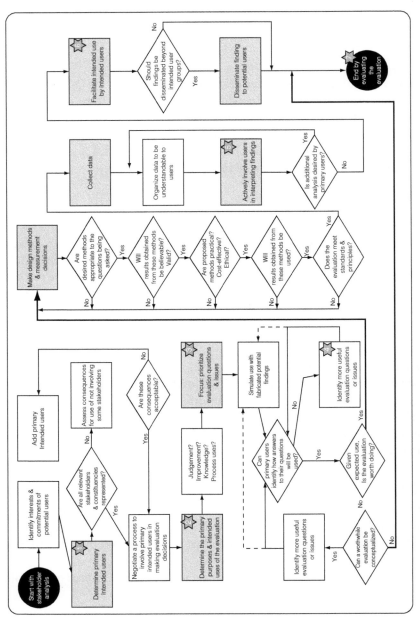

Figure 4.3 *Steps in utilization-focused evaluation*

Source: Patton (2008, pp568–569), reproduced by permission of the author and publisher; shading and numbered stars added by Crabbé and Leroy

to the professional standards of evaluation research. The evaluator should, preferably, possess communicative and negotiation skills and be familiar with all possible evaluation methods and techniques.

Besides a flowchart, Patton (1997) also compiled a checklist of focal points in the execution of a utilization-focused evaluation (see www.wmich.edu/evalctr/checklists/ufechecklist.htm).

References and Examples

Primary and additional references

Alkin, M. C. (1995) 'Lessons learned about evaluation use', Panel presentation at the International Evaluation Conference, American Evaluation Association, Vancouver, Canada

Cronbach, L. J., Ambron, S. R., Dornbusch, S. M., Hess, R. D., Hornik, R. C., Philips, D. C., Walker, D. F. and Weiner, S. S. (1980) *Toward Reform of Program Evaluation*, Jossey-Bass, San Francisco, CA

Davis, H. R. and Salasin, S. E. (1975) 'The utilization of evaluation', in E. L. Struening and M. Guttentag (eds) *Handbook of Evaluation Research, vol 1*, Sage, Beverly Hills, CA

Joint Committee on Standards for Educational Evaluation (1994) *The Program Evaluation Standards: How to Assess Evaluations of Educational Programs*, Sage, Thousand Oaks, CA

Joint Committee on Standards for Educational Evaluation (1981) *Standards for Evaluations of Educational Programs, Projects, and Materials*, McGraw-Hill, New York, NY

Patton, M. Q. (1980) *Qualitative Evaluation Methods*, Sage, Beverly Hills, CA

Patton, M. Q. (1982) *Practical Evaluation*, Sage, Beverly Hills, CA

Patton, M. Q. (1994) 'Developmental evaluation', *Evaluation Practice*, vol 15, no 3, pp311–319

Patton, M. Q. (1997) *Utilization-Focused Evaluation: The New Century Text*, 3rd edition, Sage, Thousand Oaks, CA

Patton, M. Q. (2008) *Utilization-Focused Evaluation*, 4th edition, Sage, Thousand Oaks, CA

Stufflebeam, D. L. (2001) 'Evaluation models', *New Directions for Evaluation*, no 89

Examples

Michael Patton has applied his approach to various policy fields in the US, including education, healthcare and psychiatrics, justice, agriculture, energy policy, community-building, poverty alleviation, housing, etc. He has worked with U-FE at a local and a regional scale, but also at the level of US states, as well as at national and international levels. He describes a number of examples in Patton, M. Q. (2002) *Qualitative Research and Evaluation Methods*, 3rd edition, Sage, Thousand Oaks, CA.

Briedenhann, J. and Butts, S. (2005) 'Utilization-focused evaluation', *Review of Policy Research*, vol 22, no 2, pp221–243

Governments, in both developed and less developed nations, promote rural tourism as an instrument of socio-economic development. Tourism scholars highlight the use of evaluation as a tool in managing the development of tourism. Despite this, few evaluation studies appear to form an integral part of tourism development practice. The importance of evaluation lies not only in its technical correctness, but also in how the evaluation results are used. The emphasis on the use of evaluation findings in the utilization-focused evaluation approach suggested by this article is congruent with this contention.

Davis, M. V. (2006), 'Teaching practical public health evaluation methods', *American Journal of Evaluation*, vol 27, no 2, pp247–256

Human service fields, and more specifically public health, are increasingly requiring evaluations to prove the worth of funded programmes. Many public health practitioners, however, lack the required background and skills to conduct useful and appropriate evaluations. During the late 1990s, the US Centers for Disease Control and Prevention created the Framework for Program Evaluation in Public Health to provide guidance and promote the use of evaluation standards by public health professionals. The emphasis of the framework is utilization-focused evaluation for programme improvement or to assess programme impact.

Index

For Product Safety Concerns and Information please contact our EU
representative GPSR@taylorandfrancis.com
Taylor & Francis Verlag GmbH, Kaufingerstraße 24, 80331 München, Germany